Hard-Nosed Advice from a Cranky Law Professor

Hard-Nosed Advice from a Cranky Law Professor

How to Succeed in Law School

Austen L. Parrish
Vice-Dean for Academic Affairs
and Professor of Law
Southwestern Law School

Cristina C. Knolton
Associate Professor of
Legal Analysis, Writing and Skills
Southwestern Law School

CAROLINA ACADEMIC PRESS
Durham, North Carolina

Library of Congress Cataloging-in-Publication Data

Parrish, Austen L.
Hard-nosed advice from a cranky law professor : how to succeed
in law school / Austen L. Parrish, Cristina C. Knolton.
        p. cm.
Includes bibliographical references and index.
ISBN 978-1-59460-802-5 (alk. paper)
    1. Law--Study and teaching--United States. 2. Law students--
United States--Handbooks, manuals, etc. I. Knolton, Cristina C.
II. Title.

    KF283.P37 2010
    340.071'173--dc22

                                                        2010005209

Carolina Academic Press
700 Kent Street
Durham, North Carolina 27701
Telephone (919) 489-7486
Fax (919) 493-5668
www.cap-press.com

Printed in the United States of America
2019 Printing

for Leslie, Natalie, and Amelie
AP

for my Papa Joe
CK

Summary of Contents

Contents

Acknowledgments

We are grateful to those who read and commented on this book during its many drafts, and for the support of Southwestern Law School. Special thanks to our Southwestern colleagues for their ideas and encouragement. And, lastly, thanks to our students, including Eric Geier, Elliot Jung, Brian Luper, Para Noh, and Jessica Priel for their research assistance, and Lisa Dennis, Courtney Martin, and Natalie Rodriguez for their suggestions.

Introduction

The idea of approaching law school in a traditional manner is out of vogue. No one right way exists, or so we are told, on how to learn. Students have many different perspectives, depending on their cultural and economic background, as well as where, when, and in what order they were born. Students are often advised that the path to success changes depending on whether they are a Baby Boomer, a Tweener, a Gen Xer, or a Gen Yer. For many then, the way to achieve success in law school is a personal thing. Students are encouraged to do whatever they feel most comfortable with and to embrace what works for them. Each student has their own way of doing well, and every rule can be bent or broken.

This book takes a different approach. It provides no-nonsense, sometimes hard-nosed, advice that is intended to cut across generations. Students learn in different ways. But regardless of a student's background, law professors expect specific things. A student either figures out what the professor wants, or is left behind. Doing what "is comfortable" or what "works for you" is bad advice because when students begin law school they have no idea what works, and the first year of law school is not a comfortable experience. In short, if a student wishes to excel, there *are* right ways to approach law school. This book explains—hopefully in a humorous way—what some of those ways are.

What follows are a series of essays intended to help students understand what law professors expect of them. Written by a cranky, cantankerous professor at the fictional Prynceton Law School, the essays do not mince words. In a grumpy, but straight-talking fashion, each essay instructs students on how to give themselves the best chance of doing well. The essays cover those tasks that students commonly face in law school: from reading and briefing cases, to outlining, to preparing and taking exams, to being called on in class. The book also provides advice on success outside the classroom. In many ways, the book promotes professionalism and common sense.

This book distinguishes itself in two ways. First, many law school preparation guides are hundreds of pages long and purport to anticipate every tidbit of information an aspiring law student might wish to know, no matter how tangential. Few students read those books cover to cover. And the advice they provide is often, at best, only marginally useful. In contrast, this is a short book. It is not, and is not intended to be, an exhaustive guide to all things law-school related. It attempts to be concise and to-the-point: an accessible book that can be read quickly. Second, the advice that some preparation books provide is gimmicky. Student are told they can succeed only if they master some closely-guarded secret, which law professors know but conspiratorially refuse to reveal. This book rejects that sort of nonsense. Students succeed in law school not through short cuts and tricks, but through hard work. Instead of peddling gimmicks, this book provides concrete advice on those near-universally agreed upon fundamentals that students must master to do well.

A final point. The authors are not suggesting that professors should be curmudgeonly and cantankerous or seek to emulate this book's jaded professor. The book is not an instruction guide for how professors should teach. In the vein of Kingsfield, Perini, and other caricatures of tough instructors, our jaded professor has been teaching just a little too long. Most law professors these days are a little more humane in their approach. But our crusty professor has sound advice that, if heeded, can help students succeed.

Hard-Nosed Advice from a Cranky Law Professor

Chapter 1

Preparing for Law School

Prynceton law school has an "Introduction to Law School" course. It meets during the summer. It was there that I first met Professor Lawrence. I was eager to meet him. He was a professor who would teach one of my doctrinal courses in the Fall. Today would be my first glimpse of what I was in for.

It was 8:59 a.m. when he strode in and walked, mostly unwavering, to the front of the class. He didn't seem much of a professor. He was of medium build and height, and his body showed signs of age. His skinny legs seemed lost in his clothes, his hands were delicate and boney, and his hair, peppery white, was shortly trimmed. It was hard to say his exact age. For me, having just turned 22, I would have guessed he was somewhere between 70 and 150.

He seemed out of place in the recently renovated law school. You could have more easily imagined him in an older building, in a room with dark paneling and velvety wallpaper. And I suspect that he would have been more comfortable with chalk, a cigarette, and two fingers of scotch, than the markers, laptop computer, and document camera we could see next to the podium. Certainly the clothes he wore suggested a man of an earlier time. The tweed jacket he had on was last in style sometime in a prior century. And whether by virtue of his clothes or the way he carried himself, I could not say, but he gave off the dour impression of a man who is sometimes crusty and difficult. There was something about him that made everyone else in the room seem somewhat under-sized and trivial.

As he surveyed the class, he looked a little bored, maybe even disappointed. He removed his black-rimmed glasses and began to speak. We couldn't help but listen....

Getting Ready for the First Year

"Welcome. So you think you want to go to law school. Good. I like seeing new faces. Students keep me feeling young. In the next hour, I will tell you what law school is all about; what you need to do to get ready. Listen carefully. Getting off to a good start is critical.

A. A Little Perspective

You need to be prepared for law school, but perhaps not in the way you suspect. Students are now told (or so it seems) that they must do many things before the first day of class: from reading law books and outlining cases, to perusing legal philosophy, to reading classics, like *Bleak House*. Absolute nonsense. Your entire undergraduate education is your preparation. A few months of futzing around playing "lawyer" is not going to do anything for you.

The school's Admissions Committee believed you were ready for law school or you would not have been admitted. They were willing to take you as you are. They had confidence in you. You should too. The last few months before law school is not the time to run around half-cocked trying to get ahead.

Relax. Yes, that is what you need to do the summer before you start law school. The first year of law school can be stressful. You will be asked to do a tremendous amount of work. You will be pushed harder mentally than you have before (for some of you, based on the sorry state that colleges are in, being pushed less would be a challenge!). So relax. Take advantage of the time you have left. Hit the beach. Spend time with family. Kick back. Do not read casebooks. Do not read legal philosophy. Do not read law books. If you want to read something, read the latest vampire love story (or whatever you kids are into these days). Maybe a good harlequin romance. That's good prep. That has a much better chance of helping you. In fact, reading a popular book is a good idea. Much of what you do in law school is read. You will need to read more than you have before and getting into the habit of reading every day is good practice.

Before I forget, another small point. Do not e-mail me or your other professors in the summer to introduce yourself and explain how lucky we are to have you in class. It may surprise you, but we don't need to be regaled with your many wondrous accomplishments, as spectacular as I'm sure they are. Professors are busy and they don't need stalkers. Don't worry. You will have plenty of time to kiss-up to the faculty once the school year begins.

B. Use the Summer Before Wisely

There are a few things that are essential to do before law school. First, despite my earlier advice, if your school offers a legal writing course or an introduction to law school course over the summer, take it. Many incoming students find these courses helpful. Schools often design these courses to give students a leg up before they arrive. Some schools will offer a summer academic support program, where a professor will explain how to brief cases, create outlines, and participate in class. If you have the opportunity to take this kind of course, seize the opportunity. It will make your transition from college to law school easier.

Second, and more importantly, get your personal life in order. The start of law school is not the time to be tying the knot, getting divorced, starting a new relationship, buying a house, or making any other major life decisions. If you are moving to a new city, be sure to arrive ahead of time to get settled. Have you figured out your housing? Is it relatively near the school? Is it in a safe area? You will be busy. You do not want to be commuting long distances, if you can help it. If you can live on campus, live there. You don't need to spend a lot of money. You're still a student, not a Wall Street investment banker. Don't worry, you can move up to sweeter digs after you graduate.

C. Prepare Your Family and Friends

You want to prepare your family and friends for the upcoming year. The first year of law school requires sacrifices. Life exists outside of law school, but you also need to ensure your loved ones realize that you are going to be busy. Taking an entire week off right before exams to go home for Thanksgiving, for example, is a bad idea. And you can't take your boyfriend or girlfriend out every night—you'll be studying. You will not have the time to do all the things you once did.

How do you prepare your family? Have them visit the law school. If there's an orientation, invite them to join you. If you can, have them to sit in on a class. Make them read one of the cases. If they did not go to law school, give them a glimpse of what law school is like—a taste of what you have to go through each day. Tell you what, bring them to my class. I'll scare the heck out of them. By the time I'm finished, they'll be sending you home-baked cookies, family-care packs, and doing your laundry on a weekly basis.

D. Visit the School

You want to hit the ground running, so you might as well visit the school too. Get the lay of the land. Figure out where your classes are. If you think far enough ahead, you can even sit in on a class. Find out where the library is, and the key administrative offices. Talk to the school's admissions office and ask them for a tour of the school. They are sure to give you one, and it may make the first few days of school easier.

E. Work Out Your Finances

You want to be able to focus on one thing your first year of law school: the first year of law school. You can not afford to be distracted by worrying about your finances. So—unless you are one of the very few who are independently wealthy and can just write a check to pay for your education—before law school begins set up a meeting with the school's Financial Aid Office. You will want to apply for Financial Aid, scholarships, grants and to anyone that is willing to give you money.

Law school is expensive. If you paid for your undergraduate education while working, you're going to have sticker-shock. The cost of legal education recently has skyrocketed. By the time you are finished with law school, you may be over $150,000 in debt. Don't worry. That's just the way it is. You are making an investment. It may take you a long time, but you'll pay it back. Law school isn't cheap, but if you use some common sense it does not have to force you into bankruptcy.

Approach law school frugally. You are a student, so live like a student. Create a budget and live as leanly as possible. You should not be enjoying the high-life, traipsing to school in Manolo Blahniks or Jimmy Choos. Please, get real. No matter how riveting you look in that Armani suit, or how you think having that Dolce Gabanna bag will totally transform you—don't be an idiot. That pizza you buy today will be a $1,000 by the time you pay it back in ten years (okay, maybe interest rates are not that steep, but they're steep enough). Be thrifty. Be wise. Get a roommate. Buy used books. Get a lower-rent apartment. Eat in more, eat out less. Keep that old junker of a car, you don't need a new one. You'll thank yourself later.

While I'm on the topic of stupidity. Credit cards are not a wise method for paying for law school tuition. Credit card interest rates are high, and you will almost always need to start paying them off while you're still in school. Because of the way credit car payments work, you also are at a higher risk of ruining your credit. Speak with your Financial Aid Office at your school, they can explain your options. Using credit cards is not one of them.

The Right Mindset

To do well in law school, you need to understand what getting a juris doctor (JD) is all about. Here are the basics.

A. Understand the Point of Law School

When you begin law school, it's helpful to understand what law school is all about and, more importantly, what law school is not about. Law school is not intended to teach solely to the bar exam. If your law school is too focused on the bar exam—transfer. The bar exam has little to do with long-term career success, and you don't want to be in a school that is obsessed with teaching to it. If you want to learn what they test on the bar exam, take a bar exam preparation course. Bar exam preparation courses are much cheaper than coming to Prynceton.

In many ways, law school also is not primarily designed—at least not the first-year courses—to teach you how to become a practicing attorney. Not directly. Most first-year courses are structured to teach you how to do legal analysis, how to read and understand cases and statutes, and how to think creatively, in a sophisticated way, about legal issues. That's it. And, believe me, that is more than enough. In the upper-division, you will have more opportunities to take courses that teach you practical lawyering skills and the ins-and-outs of legal practice. The best schools—and when I say best, I don't mean highest-ranked—will provide you instruction in the upper-division on how to do those tasks that young attorneys most commonly face, from document drafting, to negotiation, to oral advocacy, to client interviewing and counseling.

Law school is also not primarily intended to teach you the law. Your expression is telling; you don't believe me. But it's true. In class, you will discuss the law, sure. But the primary purpose of discussing the law is the discussion itself, that is the give and take, the pros and cons, the creative thinking, and the ability to think around and beyond the facts of the case at hand. The process of thinking through and arguing the issues is what class is for. In class you will explore the historical development of the law, the policies that underlie it, and how law reflects fundamental assumptions about ourselves, our society, and our culture. Ultimately, what most professors test for in exams is not some "right" answer, but your ability to do the very kind of analysis involved in class discussions. Law school tests your ability to think through issues presented by the cases and statutes, and to exercise your own judgment about them.

Nor is law school mostly about memorizing black-letter law. You'll be tempted to think it is. You'll be wrong. Black-letter law are those principles in a particular area or field of law (for example, contracts or torts) that are beyond dispute. Black-letter law is rarely useful in practice. Lawyers do not fight over legal principles that are free from doubt. Lawyers fight over cases when the law is uncertain. If you want to learn black-letter law, become a legal secretary. Anyone can pick up a simple statute and read it. But no client pays for a lawyer who spits back only what any fool could look up for themselves. Being a lawyer requires more. If you want to learn how to challenge the law, how to figure out answers to questions when no law exists, how to develop creative solutions for clients—then you are in the right place.

B. Question Everything

Question everything. Getting in the right mindset means that you will question everything that you read and hear in law school. If you're not questioning, you are not thinking. If you are not thinking, you are not learning. And if you are not learning, you might as well go home.

When I say "question everything," I do not mean you should constantly raise your hand. Sure participate, but do it selectively. No one likes a show-off. But don't accept everything your professor says or read your casebooks like a mindless automaton. Think about what is being said. Do you agree? Why? Why not? Is the legal principle you are studying a good one? Who does it benefit? Who doesn't it benefit? What are the law's implications? Why is it the law? Should it be? How does the case demonstrate law in practice? I like students who question what they hear and read. Those students will make good lawyers.

C. Accept Ambiguity

In law school, you must accept ambiguity. Often there is no right answer. Don't misunderstand me. There are wrong answers; lots of them. Students consistently give wrong answers when they have not read the material carefully or have failed to understand what they have read. But many right answers exist. Get used to professors not telling you the answer. They are not being mean. They are not hiding the ball. One right answer rarely exists. It's the nature of law. The best students and the best lawyers understand this. Cases are what you make of them, and so too is the law. You use it for the ends you need it for.

D. Understand the Socratic Method

I probably should say a word or two about the Socratic method. Ah, the Socratic method: the bane of every law student's existence. The one thing that sends shivers through and strikes fear in even the most accomplished of students.

What is the Socratic method? In its classic form, a professor questions students to more fully understand the topic at hand. The professor will ask questions until a contradiction is exposed in the student's reasoning, thereby proving a fallacy in the student's initial assumptions. To learn an area of law through Socratic discourse, the area is broken down into a series of questions, the answers to which gradually distill information about that area of law. Or, more simply: the Socratic method means lots of questioning and not much lecturing.

Most law professors no longer use the Socratic method, at least not as classically understood, and not in its severe form. Many modern professors are worried that they are being too hard on their students, and don't want to make them feel uncomfortable. To that I say, "cry me a river." Life's tough and students are better off if they know that right now. In any case, the so-called Kingsfield-approach that involves humiliating students has long been out of fashion. The contemporary approach is more of a conversation. Law professors these days use class discussions and light questioning as a way to engage students in a large class and explore difficult and complicated legal issues. Asking students questions and probing their understanding of the material is intended to help develop students' critical thinking skills. Questioning students forces students to analyze legal issues, to reason, and then to think critically about not only their own arguments, but also those made by others. It requires students to be well-prepared and to have read carefully before class. The professor is also forcing the student to articulate, develop, and defend a position that may at first be just an intuition. Professors also try to connect legal reasoning to professional and moral values.

So how does it work. Generally, the professor invites a student to summarize a case assigned for that day's class. Professors will also often ask students, as a way to get the discussion started, to summarize either the facts, issues, holding, or reasoning of the court's decision. Professors expect a cogent and succinct summary. Regardless of the thoroughness of the student's initial response, the professor then pushes the student on details perhaps overlooked or on issues unresolved. A professor will often manipulate the case's facts into a series of hypotheticals and then ask a student whether the court should have ruled differently if the case's facts changed slightly.

Once you understand the purpose of law school, the Socratic method (or modern variations on it) makes sense. One of law school's primary goals is to equip students with the analytical skills they need to solve legal problems. The law changes and the legal issues students will confront after they graduate can vary tremendously. Teaching students particular pieces of law is of limited value. What professors can do well is help students develop those legal reasoning skills that will aid students when they become lawyers, regardless of the area of practice.

E. Cautiously Use Hornbooks and Commercial Outlines

Hornbooks and treatises contain comprehensive and in-depth discussions of particular areas of the law. Commercial outlines, in contrast, are guides that cover the specific cases and legal rules typically covered in your courses. Commercial outlines present the material in a condensed fashion and are often designed to mirror the material included in the casebook.

You should use hornbooks, treatises, and commercial outlines, but sparingly. Some people will tell you to buy them right away. Perhaps a second-year student. Maybe your parents. They don't know what they are talking about. You will not buy them right away. You will wait. You will struggle with the material. You will force yourself to read the difficult cases. If you don't, you are short-changing yourself. You are training your brain to take the shortcuts.

This does not mean that hornbooks, treatises, and commercial outlines don't have their uses. They are great for filling in the gaps, and if you're confused in a class, you need to figure out the answer. If that means going to the library and finding a book that explains what you're covering in class, so be it. But do not kill trees and break your backs. You've got enough to read without reading other unassigned material. I don't know how many times I've seen students lug around stacks and stacks of supplemental materials. That makes me smile. Those students are done for.

F. Create a Schedule

The most important piece of preparation advice I can give you is to get organized. You want to plan out how you're going to spend your days and weeks. You should include in your schedule time for reading, briefing cases, reviewing class notes, preparing for class, outlining, meeting with professors, and taking practice exams. When the semester starts, you should be spending most of your time reading, briefing, and getting ready for class. As the semester ends, you should spend most of your time finishing your outlines and taking practice exams.

During law school, with class time and studying combined, you should be working a full 8–9 hours each day during the week. With lunch and other breaks, that means you're likely putting in a 9–11 hour day. If you can't handle that, then the legal profession may not be right for you. Although not all jobs are this way, many young lawyers regularly work 10–12 hour days, and some many more. The reality is the practice of law is challenging and the economic pressures and deadlines can commonly lead to lost weekends and evenings.

G. Avoid Common Missteps

To succeed in law school also be sure to avoid common missteps. First, the most common mistake made by new students is to view the process as a competition with classmates. Compete only with yourself. Your classmates are your allies and they will certainly be your future colleagues. The legal community is small, and you begin building your reputation when law school begins. Share your outlines. Share your notes. Don't hoard library materials. You want to be respected, not hated.

Second, you want to manage stress. This means you should strive for balance. Law school requires a lot of work, but it doesn't mean you should try to study twenty-four hours a day, seven days a week. There will be many ups and downs for you in the first year, and some of you will hit times of self-doubt. But there's more to life that just law school. You can't go through life as a machine. If you like exercising, continue exercising. Be sure to eat right. Get enough sleep and don't completely tune out your friends and family. In fact, make new friends. Loved ones are a natural support system for law school stress. While most friends and family, unless they are lawyers themselves, will not understand how difficult law school can be, they can provide support.

Of course, there are other ways to guarantee failure: not attending class, not outlining, not doing practice questions, and relying too heavily on commercial outlines. Don't worry. We'll talk more about those things later.

Understanding the First-Year Curriculum

The first-year courses are all foundational. For most schools and most JD programs, you will have no choice in your schedule. You must take the courses they tell you. And no matter what school you're attending, the first year courses are likely to be the same: Torts, Criminal Law, Contracts, Civil Procedure, Property, and Legal Writing. So what are they? Here's a very brief overview.

A. Civil Procedure

Civil Procedure is designed to acquaint students with the stages of civil litigation. At its core, civil procedure is about litigation—a dispute often between private individuals or entities. Unlike a criminal case, where the government initiates proceedings against a defendant who has allegedly violated the law, civil litigation is generally aimed at vindicating private rights. In civil litigation a plaintiff sues a defendant seeking a remedy. The Civil Procedure course examines the rules that govern the civil litigation process. For most schools, the focus is on the rules that govern the federal courts, known as the Federal Rules of Civil Procedure, as well as relevant constitutional and statutory provisions.

B. Contracts

The Contracts course addresses how legal binding agreements are made, and what makes particular promises or agreements legally binding. In other words, Contracts examines the formation, performance, and breach of written and oral agreements. The course will likely examine how to dissolve a contract, and the remedies available for breach of contractual obligations. Often the course will examine the challenges that exist to contract law, including questions as to the law's fairness and certainty.

C. Criminal Law

Criminal law teaches the law of crimes and the defenses to those crimes. The course explores a body of statutory and common law that deals with crimes and the legal punishment for criminal offenses. What constitutes burglary? Murder? Theft? You'll also study inchoate offenses, such as accessory, attempt, and conspiracy. And you'll likely study the objectives behind enforcement of criminal laws, including punishment, rehabilitation, and restitution. The course will usually focus not only on court decisions, but also on model codes and statutory law. (What? You don't know what an inchoate offense is? That's not my problem. Buy a dictionary. Look it up. I don't have time to teach you English as well as law!)

D. Property

In Property, students study the law governing the ownership and transfer of personal and real property. More broadly, property law governs relationships among people with respect to things. Topics covered in a first-year Property course include personal property, estates and interests in land, landlord-tenant, basic land conveyancing, and private land use controls. (Good, I see you're learning. Look up *conveyancing* too.)

E. Torts

Torts is the study of wrongful acts. Your Torts course will include analysis of liability for personal injuries and injuries to property. The course focuses on civil-court cases and the rational for imposing civil liability on a party for harm done to another. The law of negligence usually occupies a central place in the course, but you will also consider topics such as strict liability, liability of producers and sellers of products, nuisance, and liability for defamation and invasion of privacy. Considering the need for victim compensation as a societal issue, a Torts course often considers alternatives to the tort system—such as no-fault systems.

F. Legal Research and Writing

Legal Research and Writing is a course that will teach you how to write lawyerly documents, often legal memorandum or briefs, and how to research the law. Learning to write like a lawyer is perhaps one of the greatest challenges you'll face in law school. Putting aside rare exceptions, you can not be an effective lawyer without being a good writer. Most schools will have you take a course to help you develop and improve the skills necessary to produce high-quality legal writing. In an increasing number of law schools, the course also teaches basic lawyering skills, beyond research and writing, and provides concentrated instruction on legal methods, legal reasoning, and legal processes.

Well that's all for now. If you've paid attention, you'll do fine. See you in class. I look forward to it."

* * * * *

He then walked out, as quickly as he had arrived. On reflection, that was a little intense. I just realized how much I had to do before law school began!

Okay, here's what I'd written down in my notes from the lecture:

To Do the Summer Before

☐ Visit law school, sit in on class
☐ Take summer introduction courses if available
☐ Work out housing (not too costly, close to school)
☐ Get personal life in order
☐ Prepare family and friends for busy year
☐ Meet with Financial Aid Office and arrange finances (apply for scholarships, if not too late)

To Remember in Law School

☐ Be inquisitive
☐ Be prepared every day
☐ Accept ambiguity
☐ Use hornbooks, treatises, and commercial outlines very sparingly (don't buy right away)
☐ Create a schedule for the Fall semester (study time, class prep., classes etc.)
☐ Be supportive of classmates, not competitive (future colleagues)
☐ Strive for balance (i.e., eat, exercise)—but will be working very hard!

In a few weeks I would see Professor Lawrence again when law school started. If first-impressions meant anything, Professor Lawrence's course was going to be interesting....

Chapter 2

Briefing Cases

Well, my prediction had been right. Prynceton Law was a good school, but by no means did that mean it was a comfortable and agreeable place. And Professor Lawrence's course was less agreeable than most. We had only just started the first week of the semester and already we were sensing that Professor Lawrence was not your usual warm and cuddly professor. He was something else....

Take what happened yesterday. About five minutes into class, Professor Lawrence caught eye contact with a student at the very back of the class, Rick James. The poor schmuck.

"Mr. James, tell us the facts of *Rochester v. Smithe.*"

"Well, the court held...," Rick sputtered only a few words before Lawrence cut him off.

"No. I want the facts. Not the holding. I want the facts." Lawrence said calmly. He then raised an eyebrow. "Mr. James, do you know what facts are?"

"Yes, sure. The facts are those details ..."

"Mr. James, stop. That was a rhetorical question. I don't need you to answer rhetorical questions." Lawrence scanned the room. It looked like he was done with Rick. He seemed to be looking for his next victim. And then he found her—Julie Nguyen. "Ms. Nguyen, please help save Mr. James and the rest of us. What are the facts of this case?"

"Oh, um, in *Rochester*, the plaintiff appealed after the lower court...."

"No. Facts. Not procedure. Facts. Just Facts." Lawrence, although still speaking calmly, was pacing slowly, deliberately. "Let's try this a different way. Ms. Nguyen, where is your case brief?"

"Oh, right here." She pointed to her laptop computer. Lawrence did not look impressed. This wasn't going to be pretty.

"Ms. Nguyen. Do not treat me as an idiot. That is not a case brief. That is a computer. Does a computer look like a piece of paper?"

"Uh, no. Of course not."

"Then why are you telling me that your computer is your case brief? Briefs are written or typed on paper. I'm sure you have plenty of other wonderful things on your nifty laptop. But it's not a brief. If the brief is on your computer and not in your hand, it is useless to you. Come to class prepared Ms. Nguyen. Who has a case brief? Anyone?"

"You." Lawrence pointed at Rupa Martinez. Three victims in under three minutes. Lawrence was moving fast today. "Where is your case brief?" Rupa pulled out some papers.

Professor Lawrence walked slowly up to Rupa. He picked up her brief, and thumbed through it. There must have been at least eight or nine pages of meticulously prepared notes. From where I was sitting I could see the title, *Rochester v. Smithe*, smartly typed right at the top of the page. Lawrence weighed the paper in his hand, smiled somewhat grimly (perhaps it was more of a smirk), and then put it back down. He drummed, thoughtfully, on the top of the stack with his fingers before he spoke again.

"Ms. Martinez, I need a brief. A brief is short—one or two pages at most. It's why they call it a 'brief.' If I wanted ten pages, I would have asked for a 'long.' But I asked for a brief. Not a 'long.' Not a 'book.' Not a 'treatise.' But a brief."

"Enough. Close your books. I can see I need to teach you how to prepare for class. I will explain how to brief a case. This may be the most important hour of class you will have all year. Pay attention."

"One of the skills you will master this year is how to brief a case. As you know, for this and all your first-year courses, you have been assigned a casebook. Casebooks contain edited portions of judicial decisions (i.e., cases). In class, professors like me will grill you on what those cases mean. Each case represents one small rule in a larger body of law. By constructing how that small rule relates to the law generally, you learn not only the law but also the process of legal reasoning.

A case brief is a way to be prepared for that grilling. But briefing the cases you read is important for another reason. It teaches you how to read the critically, by breaking the case into its component parts. You will brief. You will not come to my class unless you have a brief for each case I assign you to read. From now on, here's how you will do it.

The Basics

Let's start with the basics, and how and why you will write case briefs.

A. A Case Brief Defined

What is a case brief? As its name suggests, it is a short summary of the different components of the cases you read. A brief is nothing more than a study tool: a set of notes, organized in a specific, methodical way, to identify what the case is about and why it was decided in a particular way. A brief is usually no more than one page long.

Be careful not to be confused. Lawyers also use the term "brief" to refer to a legal memorandum filed in support of a motion or an appeal that presents a legal argument. That sort of brief is formal. Legal briefs are used to persuade a court to do something. You will learn about legal briefs in your first-year legal writing course. That is not the type of brief I am talking about.

B. Why You Will Brief

A case brief is useful for several reasons. It will help you understand the material, prepare for class, and complete an outline. Rewriting and summarizing material leads to better comprehension. And, perhaps most importantly, a brief helps you distill a case down to its important parts. Doing so allows you to understand and remember key components of a case—particularly helpful when you are being called on in class.

Cases have a unique structure and method to them that is different from other kinds of writing. When you first begin law school, you will find cases difficult to read and understand. Briefing a case calls upon your analytical reading ability and helps you train yourself to read and understand cases more quickly. This is important. By dissecting a case into its component parts, you improve your legal analysis and legal reasoning skills.

Upper division students will often give you bad advice. They will tell you that briefing takes too much time; that briefing does not help you do well on your exams; that briefing is not essential to class preparation. You will ignore them. Of course, some students may do well on exams without briefing. But you are not briefing solely to prepare for the exam. And, more importantly, you will not know if you are one of those students who can do well without briefing until it's too late.

C. How to Use Your Case Brief

Keep your case brief on hand during class. Do not just have it on your laptop. Be sure to print out a hard copy. By the end of class, the case brief should be covered with additional notes and jottings spurred by the day's class discussion. Consider using oversized margins so you will have plenty of space to make annotations.

At the end of the week, you should review your briefs and take the information you've learned and place it in a course outline. You should synthesize the week's material into an outline and use your case briefs as a starting point for doing that. We'll talk more about outlining later.

How to Read Cases

To brief a case properly, you must first be able to read and understand the case. The difficulty is that reading in law school is different than reading in college. In college, the reading was generally straightforward and descriptive. But reading cases in law school is not like reading a textbook in college. Nor is it like reading a novel.

A. Prepare to Read

Worry about your environment. You need a place with no distractions, where you can read without interruptions. You can not read law school cases with the necessary focus while the TV is on, while you're doing laundry, or while you're on the bus. You need a quiet, distraction-free environment. Turn off your phone, disconnect the internet, and get everything you might need for the next hour or so. Also, be honest with yourself. If reading in a nice, comfy chair will lead to an inevitable nap, get a stiff, hard-back chair. If reading in the library will lead to socializing, go somewhere else.

B. Preview the Case

Previewing a case is an important first step to reading. Before you start reading the case, get a sense of where it fits into the class generally. What is the context? Where does the case fit in the casebook's table of contents or the course syllabus? What is the case likely to be about, and why is the professor assigning it now? Are you able to get an idea as to the key issues the case will be about and where it fits into the course? Placing the case in the broader context will give you a framework to work with and make the case easier to read and understand.

C. Read Carefully

After you've placed the case in context, you should read the case carefully all the way through. Do not skim. Judicial opinions are too complicated to understand from a cursory review. And you must pay attention to detail. If a sentence or a paragraph does not make sense, stop and re-read. Don't move on until you understand what you have read.

When reading a case, it is not enough to understand what the judge writing the opinion has said. You must understand why the judges chose to reach the decision they did in the way they did. Students should energetically attack the case and assess what is written. Is what the judge has said correct? What follows from this holding? How does this decision compare to other decisions? Is the case merely applying a prior rule, or creating a new one? Why is the case in the casebook?

D. Use a Legal Dictionary

When you begin law school, you are as much learning a new language as you are learning the law. You must look up words you do not understand. Even words you think you know may have a particular, if not peculiar, legal meaning. You will be tempted to gloss over words, but don't. Building your legal vocabulary is an important skill. Most of the cases that you read will be chock full of archaic terms, Latinisms, or other legalese. You may come across hundreds of new terms in the first weeks of law school. If you fail to look those terms up, you will be at a disadvantage. Professors often ask students in class what those terms mean.

An aside: using a dictionary does not mean you need to purchase a $150, leather-bound, deluxe edition of *Black's Law Dictionary*. Sure, it's impressive. It may make you feel like a real lawyer. You may be just compensating for a Napoleonic complex. But you don't need to lug around a 50-pound, 2,000-page book. A much cheaper, used, pocket edition will serve you fine.

E. Avoid Excessive Highlighting

When reading the case for the first time, avoid excessive highlighting. Highlighting can be useful for many students. But you should employ highlighting cautiously. Because students are often unsure on what details to focus on, many students end up with a book filled with yellow. That makes highlighting useless. And students who use highlighters excessively have a tendency to skim the words they are highlighting. The same is true for excessive underlining. The first time you read a case, read it through carefully and then go back and highlight or underline details you find particularly important.

F. Take Selective Notes

Just as you should be nervous about excessive highlighting, also be wary of taking too many notes (at least the first time you're reading the case). Taking some notes will keep you engaged and reading actively. But you do not have time to write essays on every case you read. Avoid filling the margins of your casebook with mindless jottings. Save the writing for when you write the case brief.

G. Keep Track of the Parties

When reading a court decision, you should keep track of the parties. In civil cases, you have a plaintiff and a defendant. The plaintiff is asserting the claim and seeking a remedy. In a criminal case, you have the government (state or federal) and the defendant.

The name of the party initiating the court action, no matter at what stage of the judicial proceedings, appears first in the legal papers. For example, if Jones sued Smith in Federal District Court (i.e., the trial court), Jones is the plaintiff and the case is known as *Jones v. Smith*. If Jones loses in the District Court, she may appeal. At that time, in the Court of Appeals, Jones (the appealing party) is referred to as the appellant and Smith becomes the appellee. The case is still known at *Jones v. Smith*. If Jones then wins on appeal and Smith successfully petitions the U.S. Supreme Court to hear the case, the name of the case will change to *Smith v. Jones*. Smith is now the petitioner and Jones is the respondent. Changes to case titles are common in criminal cases because most reach the appellate courts when a convicted defendant appeals.

H. Distinguish Kinds of Opinions

As you read, be careful to distinguish the kind of opinion you are reading. What court is deciding the case? Is it a federal or a state court? Is it a trial or an appellate court? Is this a majority, dissenting, concurring, or plurality opinion?

A majority opinion is an opinion that is agreed to by the court's majority (for the U.S. Supreme Court, usually five of nine justices). A concurring opinion agrees with the majority's disposition of the case but is written to express a particular judge's reasoning. A dissenting opinion, in contrast, disagrees with the majority's disposition and will set out the dissenting judge's reasons for disagreeing. Lastly, a plurality opinion is the opinion from a group of justices in a case where no single opinion received support from a sufficient number of justices to create a majority.

How to Brief

No one formula exists for what should be included in a case brief. The contents of a brief should vary depending on the course and the professor. But certain components are common to all briefs: the issue, the facts, the procedure, the holding, the rules, and the court's reasoning. I am going to take you through each of these parts and explain how they work. There is also an example case and case brief in Appendix B.

A. The Issue

In this section you want to identify what legal issue the court is deciding. Appellate cases, like the ones you are reading, exist for a reason. An appellate court hears a case on appeal when one of the parties believes there is a problem with the lower court's decision. You must identify what the problem is. A well written court decision will often begin by setting out the legal issue. If the court sets forth the issue, take the time to carefully phrase the issue in your own words. Note that sometimes the issue is procedural, and sometimes it's substantive. Procedural challenges deal with court rules, while substantive challenges deal with the law the court applies.

You can state the issue in many ways. Conventionally, the issue is a short, single-sentence question. If framed properly, the question may be answered with a "yes" or "no." The issue statement should convey the legal principles in play and the significant facts material to those principles. The question should be objective and not slanted in favor of one party, nor should it state a conclusion. A common way of framing a legal issue is to use an "Under ... does ... when...." format. Under [a particular law], does [a party have a particular legal obligation or legal status] when [certain legally significant facts are present]. A case brief should indicate the precise issue the court is addressing.

Let's take an example taken from a California Supreme Court case, *Perez v. Van Groningen*. Assume you are reading a case about a passenger who was injured when he fell from a tractor, while the driver was using the tractor to disk his employer's orchards (i.e., to cultivate the soil with a disk harrow). Assume also that the employer previously told the driver that no passengers were permitted to ride on the tractor. The injured passenger is suing the driver's employer for damages, but can only prevail if the injury occurred within the driver's scope of employment.

A good issue statement might read: "Under California law, does an employee act within the scope of employment when he takes an unauthorized passenger with him in performing duties assigned by his employer?" This issue statement is effective because it includes not just the specific legal issue before the court, but identifies the relevant facts as well. It is specific enough to identify what is going on in the case, yet broad enough to be applied in future cases as well.

An issue statement that included only "Was the employee acting within the scope of employment?" is abstract and omits the facts that bring to life what occurred in the case to place it in context. There are hundreds of cases about whether an employee is acting within the scope of employment and, without further information, you do not know enough to determine what this case is about. The issue is too broad to be helpful to anyone. It needs more detail. There is another reason to be specific. Broad pronouncements of law that go beyond the case's facts are not binding on courts deciding later cases (these broad pronouncements are known as dicta). Your issue must be framed in a way that incorporates both the dispositive facts and the applicable legal principles. Lastly, writing your facts in chronological order is usually best (yes, isn't it amazing how starting with first things first makes sense!).

An issue statement can, however, be too specific. For example, the following issue statement includes too many details: "Is a tractor driver acting within the scope of employment when he is asked to disk the orchards of his employer and takes his nephew along with him without his employer's permission?" This issue statement may be technically correct. But the purpose of reading cases is to use them to predict how courts will decide future cases. It is unlikely that future cases you encounter will be about tractor drivers, nephews, and disking orchards. And those facts—the relationship of the driver and the passenger—are not material to the court's decision.

Remember, more than one "right" issue statement exists. As long as your issue statement marries relevant facts and legal principles, and is clear and concise, you may word it in different ways.

B. The Facts

You should summarize the legally significant facts of the case. What happened? What gave rise to the lawsuit? What is this case all about? Do not cut and paste what is contained in the case itself. Instead simplify. Who sued who for what? What was the crime? What happened that gave rise to the lawsuit?

The facts section should be short: one or two paragraphs— maybe less. Only include those facts necessary to understand the case. This is difficult. But struggling to identify those facts that are key to the decision is important. If you understand what facts were crucial to the court's decision, you likely understand the case. Another small point: use descriptive terms rather than proper names when referring to parties. Usually it's more helpful to refer to the parties as the buyer, seller, driver, passenger etc., than Smith, Jones, Perez, etc. Once you decide how to refer to the parties, be consistent throughout your brief.

Let's return to our example of the injured passenger. The brief's facts section would include that the defendant employed the driver and that the driver's regular duties included disking the orchard. You would include that a passenger rode with the driver and that passengers were not permitted on the tractor. Finally, the facts would state that the passenger was injured. That's it. Three sentences. Keep your facts section short.

Much of the factual description set forth in the cases you read will not be relevant to the issue before the court. For example, whether the injured passenger lived with his uncle is not relevant to the case's outcome (i.e., the issue of whether the driver was acting within the scope of his employment). Similarly, what orchard disking is, where the passenger was sitting in the tractor, and the numerous details about the passenger's injuries are all irrelevant to the case's holding. Interesting facts maybe, but not legally significant to whether the driver was acting within the scope of employment. Although sometimes you may wish to include one or two descriptive facts to provide context, including too many descriptive facts will result in a case brief as long as the case itself. If a fact is not legally significant, leave it out.

C. The Procedure

Not only should you explain what gave rise to the lawsuit, you should also briefly explain how the case came before the appellate court. Summarize what happened in the lower courts. The brief should identify the courts that have made rulings in the case and how those rulings have led to the appeal. For example, in a criminal case, was the defendant convicted? Was there a trial? In a civil case, was the defendant found liable? Was there a trial? Did a party file a motion? What kind of motion? How did the lower court rule? Who appealed?

In our tractor-injury example, the passenger filed suit against the employer. There was then a jury trial and the jury returned a verdict in the employer's favor. The passenger appealed arguing that the court should have instructed the jury that the driver was acting within the scope of employment. These are the procedural facts. They are not what actually happened to cause the injury, but what happened in court after the plaintiff filed suit.

D. The Rules

In an appeal, a court will apply a particular rule of law or standard to reach a result. The court will set forth a legal framework within which to analyze the case's facts. For the rules section of your brief, you need to determine what rule or legal principles the court applied. Sometimes rules are directly taken from a statute or code. Be careful, however, because often the rule the court applies is a common law rule that defines one of the elements set forth in the statute. In fact, many cases will not even mention a statute at all. Sometimes the rule will be a test or a set of factors a court must apply.

Often there are several different rules in one case. Sometimes there are several issues the court is addressing and each issue will have its own rules. Even if there is only one issue before the court, the case will often set forth multiple rules in its analysis of that issue. Sometimes the different rules are merely part of one larger rule or set of principles. Often a court will set forth the same rule but use a variety of different ways of saying the same thing. You need to first identify the rules that apply to the specific issue the court is addressing and then combine them into one concise rule statement that can be inserted into your brief. Sometimes to help with understanding, it is better to paraphrase the legal rule, other than merely copying it verbatim.

Let's use our tractor example to illustrate. In determining whether the tractor driver was acting within the scope of his employment, the court set forth several different legal principles. First the court said that an employer is "liable for risks arising out of employment." The court further defined this rule by stating "A risk arises out of employment when an employee's conduct is not so unusual or startling that it would seem unfair to include the loss as a cost of business." The court also included the rule that "an employer will be liable if the risk was one that may fairly be regarded as typical of or broadly incidental to the enterprise undertaken." Finally, the court mentioned that if the employee substantially deviated from the duties assigned for personal purposes, the employer is not liable.

What must you do? You need to take these rules and devise a rule summary for when an employer will be liable for acts of his employee. A good strategy might be to start with the general rule that an employer is liable for risks arising out of employment. Yet this rule alone is insufficient. This rule alone does not indicate when a court will consider risks to have arisen out of employment. Thus, you should also include when a risk will be considered "arising out of employment." You should note that risks arising out of employment include risks that are typical of or broadly incidental to the duties assigned by the employer. You might also mention in your rule that employers will not be liable if the employee's act is a substantial deviation from the duties assigned.

So your rule section might state: "An employer is liable for risks arising out of employment. Risks arising out of employment include risks that are typical of or broadly incidental to the duties the employer assigns. An employer will not be liable for an employee's negligent acts when the employee substantially deviation from the duties assigned."

Keep in mind, this is just one acceptable way of phrasing the rule. Many other versions would also be correct. Just remember to include enough of the rule to understand how to apply it and remember to combine like parts together so you don't have a rule that is a page long listing every detail the court mentioned.

E. The Holding

Your brief should also precisely state the decision's holding. What did the court do? What was the outcome? What action did the court take and for which side did the court rule? Be sure to briefly summarize what the court did on the particular facts before it.

If the court rules for the injured passenger who fell off of the tractor, the holding of the court may be that the driver was acting within the scope of his employment and the company is therefore liable for the passenger's damages.

F. The Reasoning/Policy

In appellate decisions, courts will explain why they have reached the decision they did. In the reasoning section of your case brief, you should summarize the reasoning behind the court's decision.

If the court decided the driver acted within the scope of his employment, you need to know why and you need to include this in your brief. Perhaps the court found the driver was acting within the scope of employment because the driver performed an assigned task (driving the tractor while disking the orchard) and that the driver taking the passenger along with him was incidental to those duties. Whatever the reason, you need to know it so you can use it in predicting the outcome of future cases.

Avoiding Pitfalls

There are a few pitfalls to avoid when briefing a case.

A. You Will Not "Book Brief"

Book briefing is when you only take notes in the margins of your casebook. That's fine as a complement, but not as a substitute for a case brief. You should have a separate document that forces you to think about and write out the different components of the court's decision. The same is true with "highlighter briefing," where students use different color highlighters to distinguish the different parts of the case. If you like your book to look like a rainbow, that's fine. But again, it complements and should not replace a case brief. Writing out and synthesizing what you've read is an important skill to develop. Scribbling yellow across the page is something you learned in pre-school.

B. You Will Value Substance Over Style

You will not spend hours making your brief look pretty. This is not a beauty contest. A case brief is a learning tool. It should not be treated as a sacrosanct document. Of course, it should be nicely set out in a useable and easy-to-read format. But don't spend hours tinkering with how it looks. Substance is more important here. You don't get extra points for having a really nice looking brief that says nothing.

C. You Will Not Cut and Paste

Some students have a nasty habit of looking up the case online and then cutting and pasting large portions of the case's language (or worse yet, just mindlessly typing what the case says verbatim) into the case brief. Don't. A case brief is intended to force you to carefully read and analyze a case. One of the primary goals in law school is for you to teach yourself how to read complicated cases and understand the law. If you simply retype what the judge has said, you are doing an end-run around a key reason for case briefing. Strive also to keep your brief succinct (another reason not to cut and paste). This will promote comprehension and increase your ability to better prepare for classes and exams.

D. You Will Not Use a Commercial Brief

You will not use commercial outlines or commercial case summaries when briefing. These materials can be useful and can help you understand the material you are covering, but they are not a replacement for working (perhaps struggling) with the material and briefing the case yourself. No, this is not just advice for masochists. Remember the purpose of briefing: to help you to understand the different components of a case and read critically. Using a commercial outline or case summary defeats (or at least undermines) that purpose.

A related piece of advice that's hard to follow. In law school there's a nasty tendency to decide you "need" something, just because others have it. Not since junior high will you suddenly find you must have a thing, just because everyone else has it. I've seen it before—a madcap race to the bottom as everyone buys dozens of commercial outlines. If everyone else is lugging around twenty commercial outlines, perhaps you should too, you think. But you'd be wrong. You can't go through law school with the irrational fear that other students will get all the secret insights if you don't follow like a lemming. And most times, following the crowd is a poor decision. If you like the herd mentality that much, leave law school now and go work on a farm. You'll fit in nicely with the sheep and the cows.

———————

That's all. Next time I expect you to be prepared for my questions. Unless you brief, you won't be. I trust I won't have to repeat myself.

I'm done for today. Next class we'll pick up where we left off and Mr. James can tell us the facts of the *Rochester* case."

* * * * *

Well, I'm glad I'm not Rick James ... Here is my checklist from the lecture:

The Main Point

☐ I will brief or Prof. Lawrence will get me!

Reading Cases

☐ Find a quiet, distraction-free place to read
☐ Preview the case (skim it!)
☐ Read carefully and critically
☐ Use a legal dictionary
☐ Take selective notes and avoid excessive highlighting
☐ Keep track of the parties (who is the plaintiff, who is the defendant)
☐ Focus on what court is deciding the issue (trial or appellate, state or federal etc.)

To Remember When Briefing

☐ Use a standard, easy-to-read format
☐ Include at least: (1) a statement of issues; (2) facts; (3) procedure; (4) rules; (5) holding; and (6) reasoning
☐ Keep the brief short—one page or less ideally
☐ Don't book brief

☐ Don't cut and paste (must think about what I'm writing)
☐ Don't use a commercial brief
☐ Print out hard copy before going to class
☐ Annotate and make notes on the brief during class
☐ Tailor brief for class preparation and individual professor

Chapter 3

Professor Expectations

Musing of a cranky professor.... I have long secretly suspected that my students are out to get me. Not in any vast conspiracy-type way. Don't misunderstand, I'm not a loon. I do not fret that they may have some exquisitely planned plot of high-jinks, say like putting exlax in my coffee. But I do, on occasion, get a nagging feeling that my students wouldn't be all that choked up if I was to say take a horrible spill next to the lectern, throttled perhaps by my laptop computer cord. I wonder, would anyone dash to help? Or would they just sit there, softly chuckling, sniggering even, as I gurgle my last gasp. I can imagine hearing final words from somewhere in the back, *sotto voce*, "Excellent. Serves the bastard right for calling on me."

Of course, this is fantasy. Utter ridiculousness. Anyone who has ever been in my class knows it would never happen this way. No one would say anything. Talk to any law professor. The chance of anyone even looking up from their computer screen is pretty slim. Most wouldn't realize I had fallen until IM'd or tweeted by a class-mate several minutes later.

"Hey, where's Lawrence?" "Who? Oh, yeah, teacher. Not sure. Why?" "Class seems quiet." "Did you hear that?" "What?" (Sounds in the background of me thrashing around, nails clawing into the blackboard trying furiously to extricate myself from the laptop cord, strangled, frantically pleading for help.) "Nothing, thought I heard something." "You're imagining things. LOL!!!" "Isn't Jenny looking cute today ..."

And it would go on. It probably would take at least forty minutes for anyone to notice me passed out in front, my hand twitching uncontrollably—apparently a reaction common for cadavers.

I have been told the heart, like my students, is also surfing on Facebook and wouldn't realize I was kaput right away.

You think I exaggerate? Sadly, I'm not. Most days I'll say "Good morning, class" and I swear the sound of computer keyboard typing will continue inexplicably for at least a minute. Can they be typing what I say in multiple languages? Morse code? Ancient Sanskrit? "Today, we'll be talking about ..." I stop. Tap, tap, tap, tap, tap.... enough typing to fill a book. It's like living in an Aldous Huxley novel, as a hundred automatons madly peck at their keyboards. "What are you writing? Seriously. Please tell me." No answer, just tap, tap, tap. Brave new world, yeah right.

Of course, I will say this revealing only the slightest irritation; I have to maintain my professionalism. Truthfully though, I usually want to jump up and down on the desk in front of me in utter frustration and then bang my head repeatedly into the wall over and over and over until the numbness goes away. There's a stray reddish-brown mark on the back wall of my classroom. Old paint, the building maintenance has assured me. I'm not so easily duped. I know what they won't confirm: it's the blood of my predecessor. One too many bangs of the head.

Sometimes, I see signs of life. Well barely. Maybe two students will yawn. At least it's something, I think. Perhaps a second later another will start, briefly stirring before drifting back to slumber. I make a mental note when that happens. That is a student I could write a recommendation for. At least the sleepers reveal a glimmer of intelligence, unlike the remaining who continue to type nothings onto their computers. Some day I'll stop lecturing altogether. I'll just sit there, waiting. Silence. And just when all seems lost, I'll hear the dulcet tones of a can of Red Bull popping open. The natives live. I guess I'm not alone....

It's 9 a.m. I'm getting old. I need a drink. Oh well, I better get started. Today, I'm going to teach them how to be professional in class.

———————

"Law is a profession; you must act like a professional. If you do not, you will not be in my class for long. Every professor has the same rules; the same basic expectations. They may not admit it, but they do. Here are the rules. Follow them. If you do, we will get along just fine.

A. Arrive on Time

You will arrive to class on time. I will be on time. I expect you to be too. Class starts at 9:00 a.m., not 9:01 a.m.

Lawyers must arrive on time for client meetings, for court appearances, for meetings with partners. If you arrive late, you lose clients, you lose cases, you get admonished by judges, you get fired. If you can not figure out how to get to this class on time drop out of law school now. Law school is expensive. Do not waste your money or my time.

A few of you are smarter than you look. You will get here 15 minutes early. You will settle in, you will get organized, and you will review the materials we will be covering. You will sit nearer the front than the back of the classroom, so that you can easily hear and see what's happening. The idiots in the back who are internet surfing will also distract you less when you're sitting in the front. Those who arrive early will have a better chance of doing well. I will notice who comes to class early. I will be pleased.

B. Be Prepared

You will come to class prepared. You will have read the assigned reading, you will have taken notes on the assigned reading, you will have briefed the relevant cases, you will have thought about the reading, and you will be ready to participate in class discussions. If you are not prepared, you will be lost—class will be pointless. Preparation is not optional if you wish to succeed.

No excuse exists for not being prepared. Never tell me you "didn't do the reading because you were too busy." Save it. I don't need an excuse or an apology. Worse yet, never tell me that you "didn't do the reading because you were studying for Prof. X's class." When you say that, you are telling me that I am less important than another professor. You insult me if you read for other classes and not for mine. I need you to be prepared. When you're not prepared, I have to lecture. I don't like lecturing.

Reading the day's assignment once is not being prepared. Law school requires more than that. My job is not to teach the reading. Do not expect me to summarize what you have read. That is what teachers do in junior high; this is law school. Law school is for grownups. I assume you are one. You will do the reading yourself. I will then elaborate.

C. Attend Every Class

You will attend every class. The school's policy is that you must attend at least 90% of all scheduled classes or you will be administratively withdrawn. That is the school's policy, not mine. If you want to pass this course, you will attend every class.

There are narrow exceptions to this rule. When I say narrow, I mean narrow: a sudden death in the family, a car accident on the way to school, you get kidnapped at knifepoint in the middle of the night by Al Qaeda operatives. Traffic is not an excuse. Too many beers the night before is not an excuse. I understand that sometimes missing class is unavoidable. If it happens, you will get notes from a fellow student. Do not come to my office and ask me to repeat everything you missed. I'm your professor, not your private tutor.

D. Engage with Class

You will engage. Class is fifty minutes. For fifty minutes, you will focus on this class and only this class. You will not "IM." You will not e-mail. You will not "surf." You will not play silly computer games. You will not flirt with your neighbor. You will not answer your cell phone. You will not use your Blackberry, iPhone, or your iPod. You have one task for this hour and that is to focus on this class. I deserve that respect. If you cannot focus completely on this class for one hour, leave now—this profession is not for you.

Engaging with class means being willing to participate. You will learn to enjoy being called on in class. It is an opportunity to learn —the reason you are in law school. The best students are itching for me to call on them. My questions will be tough. I do not expect you to know every answer or even most of them. You may find my questions mystifying. Don't worry. That's okay, that's normal. It will get better as the year progresses. But I do expect you to try your best.

You will never "pass" in my course. Passing means that either you are unprepared or that you are unwilling to try. Both are unacceptable. I will not let you pass. Try passing and my questions will only get worse. Don't misunderstand me though. I am not impressed by the student who flails their arms around yelling "call on me, call on me—oh, oh, I know the answer." That will not make you friends. No one likes a kiss-up.

Some of you will be crafty. You will learn that volunteering when you are prepared is better than waiting for me to call on you. I am not stupid. I know this trick. But if you have talked recently in class, I am more likely to call on someone else. So be proactive. Volunteer when you can. Don't flail, just raise your hand.

E. Answer as a Lawyer Would

In this class we talk using plain, easy-to-understand language. When I ask a question, you will answer in a clear way—you will not use Latin, you will not respond with gobbledygook. You will not tell me: "The party in the first part filed a writ of attachment against the party in the second part, *inter alia*, for failing to construct the structure in which the aforementioned plaintiff resided." That's gibberish. When you speak gibberish you sound like a fool, not a lawyer. I don't care if that's what the judge wrote in the opinion. Your job is to translate what the case has said into plain language.

When I ask you to tell me the facts of a case, you will not read verbatim from your casebook. I can read. Everyone else in the room can read. You need to have thought about the case ahead of time so that you can state, in a succinct way, what happened, for what reason, and why.

F. Go to Office Hours

At times you may not understand something discussed in class. That is okay. It is to be expected. But if, after preparing carefully for and attending class you still do not understand, you will come see me in office hours. You will not wait until the end of the semester. You will come soon after the class. This rule is important. Few students go to office hours. You will go. You've paid good money to have me as a professor. Take advantage of it.

There is another reason to visit me in office hours, even if you understand the material being covered. At some point, you will need to ask me for a favor. You may need a letter of recommendation, or you would like me to serve as a job reference, or perhaps you would like to work as my research assistant. Some of you may need me to call a judge to get you an interview for a coveted clerkship. I only help and write letters for people I know. If you do not come to office hours, I will not know you. I do not recommend people I do not know. If I do not know you, I will not be able to do the favors you ask. Just getting a good grade in my class does not mean I know you.

G. Ask Only Appropriate Questions

You will ask only appropriate questions. Students regularly ask three types of questions in law school: (1) questions designed to make the professor look stupid; (2) questions designed only to make the student look smart; and (3) all other questions. Only ask type 3 questions.

If you ask inappropriate questions, trust me I will not be happy. And if I'm not happy, then you are going to be even less happy. But do not be afraid to ask questions about the material we are covering. It shows you are engaged. It shows you care. It shows you are here to learn. It shows you understand what law school is all about. I like that.

A related point: we don't like show-offs in this school. Your mommy is a famous big-time Wall Street lawyer. You graduated summa cum laude from Harvard. You are a Rhodes Scholar. You are the leader of a small island nation. Whoopee! Good for you. I don't want to hear it. Neither does anyone else. When you raise your hand in my class it is to participate or ask a question. Show-off, make enemies of your classmates, and look foolish on your own time.

H. Be Supportive, Not Competitive

Be supportive of your classmates. Law students do best when they are supportive, not when they are competitive. Share your class notes and your outlines. In the long run, you will be rewarded for your niceness. You don't need to "pay it forward"—I don't believe in that nonsense. You just need to realize that your classmates will be your future colleagues. You are building (or destroying) your professional reputation.

When a classmate has been called upon, do not roll your eyes, guffaw, or giggle. Listen carefully. They are trying hard. You could be next.

I. Take Responsibility

This may be the most important rule. You will take responsibility for your life. I am not here to babysit you. If you do not understand everything right away that's fine. That is the way law school works. You will work hard and figure it out. But do not blame me if you do not know the law by the end of the semester. That is your problem and reflects your failings, not mine.

I am constantly shocked that students think my job is to spoon-feed them the law. Wrong. You will learn the law yourself. My job is to explore the law's implications, to discuss policy, to ask the hard questions, and to make you think. I am not here to teach the bar exam, and I am not here to prepare you to be a paralegal. Law school is an intellectual endeavor. I want you to be introspective. I want you to think and challenge yourself. If you don't like it, too bad. That is the way it is.

Since I am ranting, I might as well get something else off my chest. Please do not tell me how to teach my course. I may not be the best professor, or the clearest, or the most likeable. In fact, I know I'm not. I'm pretty horrible. But unless I solicit your feedback, do not tell me what you think of how I teach. You think I should use PowerPoint? You think I should give you more hypos and model answers? You think I should lecture more? You think I should lecture less? You think I'm too Socratic? You think I have too high expectations? Good for you. Keep it to yourself. I do not know where students get off thinking they know better than me how to teach the course. I started teaching when you were just a glimmer in your mother's eye. I was hired because someone with experience thought I knew something about the law. And, at my age, I don't give a tinker's cuss how you think law school should be taught.

At the end of the semester you will have an opportunity to complete a course evaluation. At that time, you should tell the school that I was too hard on you, that the material was too complex, that I required you to read too much, that I went too quickly, that I was a luddite, or that I did not explain the law well enough. That's all fine. Don't be mean or vindictive—but provide the school with your constructive criticism and honest opinion. At the evaluation stage, you should hold my feet to the fire. Tell the administration what you liked and what you disliked. They will listen.

A final point. I don't require excessive formality, but I am not John, I am not "buddy," I'm not "yo, over here." That may sound elitist. Perhaps it is elitist. But that is also the way it is. Once you graduate, I hope we will be on a first-name basis. But that is after you graduate. Right now, let's use "Professor."

J. Professionalism Goes Both Ways

Some students think my rules are harsh. They are not. They reflect common sense and courtesy. But the courtesy goes both ways.

If you act professionally, you have the right to expect that I act professionally too. I will arrive to class on time, I will be prepared, and I will be willing to answer your questions. I will hold office hours, and I will be in my office to meet with students during those hours. My scholarship and other work is never a valid excuse for "not having time" for students. Just as you will have the courtesy of notifying me if you have to cancel an office hours appointment, I will do the same.

I will tell you my course goals and you will be told what I expect. You have the right to a syllabus that clearly sets out the assignments for the course. You have a right not to have me change the readings every day. If changes are necessary, and they may be, you are entitled to reasonable notice. My class will have some relation to the readings you were assigned. I will not make you buy a book that has no connection to material covered in the course.

I will never make inappropriate comments about my students. Derogatory statements based on your race, your ethnicity, your gender, or your age are inappropriate. The classroom is not a place for embarrassing, humiliating, or torturing students. I may be cranky, but I never go that far. I will encourage class discussion, and I will not condemn a position based solely on its political viewpoint. I will value and not ridicule your opinions and questions. Yet don't be confused by this: I am free to criticize, and will criticize, badly reasoned, or analytically flawed opinions, or those opinions based on misstatements of the law. Valuing different viewpoints is not to value wrong answers.

You also have a right to expect professionalism in how I write and grade my course exams—just as I expect professionalism from you. My exam questions will be well-written, with clear guidelines as to what I expect. I will not use silly names for the parties, or test on material that was never covered. I will provide an explanation for why I graded you the way I did, including either notes in your exam booklet, or a cut-sheet indicating how I graded. And I will return the exams to you within a reasonable time.

Hold me accountable. I insist on the highest professionalism and you should too. And this goes for all your professors. If your professors are not prepared, do not arrive to class on time, or continuously cancel office hours—talk to your professor. If he or she is unprofessional, go to the administration.

Following these rules is your obligation. A cranky professor like me never forgets. I expect much from you, and I will show disappointment when my expectations are not met. If you act professionally, I will remember you. I will treat you as an equal. I will do my best to help you succeed. I will consider you for research or teaching assistant positions. I will serve as a reference. I will write you recommendations. I will follow your career with interest. I will be an eager mentor. And years from now—when you are applying to be a judge, or seeking a partnership, or going for a promotion—I will do what I can to help. I like seeing students succeed. It makes me feel good about life. It keeps me young. It is why I like my job.

If you don't act professionally, forget it. At my age, my time is too valuable to waste on a lost cause. I'm glad we had this chance to chat."

───────────

Class ends. I quickly gather my books and plan my escape. If I could just get.... No, too slow. A student corners me. I look furtively at the back door. But there's no escaping. He's a very "special" student. The kind that demands not hand-holding, but all out figurative bear-hugs. As he approaches, I happen to notice he's wearing ... flip-flops. Flip-flops? Are you kidding me? You think I was teaching surfing in the Bahamas. But no. It's January. It's wet. It's cold. But here he is—a future leader of tomorrow—in flip flops. God help us. What's law school turning into? I should speak with the Dean. I need a sabbatical.

* * * * *

Wow, Lawrence was on fire today. Here's what I had in my notes for this class.

Class Reminders

☐ Arrive on time (arrive early!)
☐ Arrive prepared (bring brief, notes, casebook, statutory supplement, pens, pencils etc.)
☐ Don't be afraid to participate
☐ Disable the internet (no surfing, no email)
☐ Ask questions when needed (but no showing off!)
☐ Go to office hours when needed
☐ Pay attention—listen and think

Chapter 4

Outlining

Although I was loving law school in many ways, the amount of work our professors required of us was staggering. My professors' expectations were so high. When not in class, I seemed to live in the library. Not to say I was bitter, but I was starting to view Prynceton less as a school and more as a kind of detention facility with educational opportunities. Professor Lawrence's course remained the most difficult. And he continued periodically to dole out nuggets of advice in his curmudgeonly way.

Take yesterday's class. Class had only just begun when a student raised his hand and asked what sounded like an innocuous question. "Professor, we've read a number of cases, but I don't see how they tie together. I was speaking with some of my classmates. It would be really helpful if you could explain how they connect together and give us the big picture."

Lawrence paused. He looked over the edge of his glasses, at first quizzically, apparently confused. Then he smiled, a broad, mocking smile. "I'm sure it would be helpful. It would probably be helpful if I wrote your exam for you too."

"So you will...."

Lawrence cut the student off, his smile gone. "No. I will not. That's your job. Not mine." Uh oh, it sounds like a rant was coming on.

"Students these days. I imagine you've been told since you were knee-high to a grasshopper how brilliant you are. How precious. Undergraduate schools, once bastions of higher learning, now are places where everyone is above average and the slightest bit of effort—no matter how feeble—earns praise. From the look of you, I'm sure "A" grades were thrown out to anyone with a pulse. Well none of that here. You need to work. I won't do it for you. Some of you will succeed and some of you will fail. Half of you are below average. And questions like that—asking me to do the work for you—suggests you are further below average than most."

Lawrence then paused, and reflected for a second. It seemed like he was about to continue and then suddenly changed his mind.

"Okay. Perhaps that's unfair. It's not your fault that you are awash in mediocrity yet convinced you are utter geniuses. I should not be surprised that you ask for spoon-feeding. You are the victims of too much positive reinforcement. Moddle-coddled since birth. I'll give you a break. I'm not doing the work for you. Welcome to the real world. But I will tell you how to tie it all together. Close your books. This morning I will explain how to outline."

The Basics

Many students underestimate how important outlining is in law school. Before I tell you how to outline, I want to underscore why you should outline, when you should begin outlining in law school, and what you'll be outlining. I'll finish by emphasizing a few things you should avoid.

A. Why You Will Outline

You will outline because it is the process of outlining that matters. Outlining is not about the finished product. The process of outlining forces you to organize, synthesize, and understand more fully the different topics and issues you have covered in class. Outlining—done correctly—gives you a roadmap or a strategy for tackling exam questions and requires you to think methodically about the material you have covered. By struggling with the material to create an outline and then working with that outline, you will understand the material better and will be able to see the "big picture." After outlining, you should be able to identify the overarching concepts around which the course revolved, and the significant legal principles relevant to those concepts. Law school outlines are also necessary because skimming over all the material you have covered in a semester is impossible. You need some condensed way to review the material for the exam. In short, outlines are study aids.

You are foolish if you solely use commercial outlines. The only thing more foolish than solely using a commercial outline is borrowing an outline from a friend or from an upper division student, or downloading from an "outline bank" on the internet. If you're going to cut corners, you might as well do it with something reliable that an expert has written. Sure, someone has told you: "why bother doing what someone else has already done for you?" That person is an idiot. And you are an idiot if you listen to them.

Commercial outlines serve their purpose—just a purpose different than you might expect. Commercial outlines may provide a student with an overview at the start of a law school course—sort of a preview of things to come, to help you see the forest from the trees. You can also use a commercial outline when you get stuck —as a tool to help you understand the material in a way that is helpful to you. Commercial outlines can sometimes help you organize your thoughts if you are confused as to an area of the law. But they are supplements, and supplements only. They can never replace the process of creating your own outline. Doing it yourself allows you to organize, learn, and think through the material you must know for the final exam.

B. When to Outline

You will begin outlining early. Many students will wait until the end of the semester, just before exams start. You will not. In your first year of law school, you will start no later than the fourth or fifth week of a fifteen-week semester. Earlier than this, you have likely not covered sufficient material. Courses in the first year usually start out slow. After the first semester of law school, you should begin outlining in the second or third week of the semester.

Starting early is important. You cannot possibly start and finish everything you need to do in the last few weeks of the semester. In addition to outlining, you will need to complete practice exams, memorize key rules, and review the material the professors have covered. Students who wait until late in the semester to begin outlining are almost guaranteeing themselves a lower grade. Outlining early is also important because the more you go over the material the more likely you will understand it in a meaningful way.

You should create a schedule. In that schedule, set aside time each week to outline your different courses. Some students set aside Saturday or Sunday solely for outlining. Others prefer to read on the weekend, and therefore carve out a different evening of the week to outline for each course. Either way is fine. The key is to create a schedule and stick with it and update your outline each week. If you do not, getting side-tracked is easy.

C. When to Stop Outlining

A related question is when should you finish your outline? Plan to complete your outline on the last day of class (or the weekend following the last day of class). You do not want to be outlining right up to the exam. Too many students wait too long, and use up precious time right before the exam to learn the material. Outlining is a process. It helps you synthesize and understand the material discussed in class. If you've kept to your schedule and updated your outline each week, you should finish just as the course is finishing.

D. What to Outline

In law school, you will find students with massive outlines— hundreds upon hundreds of pages of material containing everything one could possibly want to know about the course's subject matter. These massive tombs will contain the student's class notes, the student's notes on the reading, the student's notes on their notes, the student's summary of commercial outlines, the student's notes on hornbooks, their notes from study group meetings, excerpts from statutes, excerpts from cases, hypothetical questions from class, and maybe even the professors musing and ramblings on various topics. These kinds of War-and-Peace Outlines make students feel warm and comfy knowing that they have transcribed everything anyone could ever want to know about a topic. The outline's author will be proud. He or she may even brag about the outline. It will become a document of worship. And it will be absolutely and completely useless.

A good outline is not an "information dump." You are not writing a treatise when you outline. Instead, an outline should be a condensed, focused, and synthesized summary of the key legal rules that you have explored through the cases read. It should provide you with a framework through which to answer exam questions—a roadmap of how to answer a legal problem, step-by-step. An outline should take each rule for a particular area of the law and then it should break that rule into its substantive elements, while noting alternative rules or approaches. It might mention policy. It might provide examples. And it will be relatively short.

An illustration may make this easier to follow. If you were to read a book about Italian baking, you might start with the history of baking in Venice, how Italian tastes changed over time, the major influences on Italian food, the different signature dishes of Italian deserts, etc. But if you are asked a specific question—"how do I make an Italian cake?"—you need a recipe; a step-by-step instruction guide. You must know to put the flour in the bowl before the eggs and in what amount. You need to know how long to bake and at what temperature. When baking a cake, it is of little help to know that the first cake was baked in 1300 B.C. This is the same for most law school courses. In class and in the readings you will likely explore the law, legal history, the policy implications behind the law, how judges decide cases, and many other things. But for most exams, you need to know step-by-step how to analyze a question. Your outline should provide you with the recipe for doing so.

E. What to Avoid

A few things to avoid when outlining. As an initial matter, do not get bogged down with case names and minute details of cases.

Most professors do not require that sort of detail. The goal of law school is not to have you memorize thousands of inconsequential, nit-picky facts. Instead, you need to know the elements of the rules. An outline necessarily removes legal nuances and fact specific distinctions in cases, and forces you to think of general legal principles.

Do not get hung up with formatting. An outline is a tool for you to understand the material. Sure, it must be organized. It should be readable and easy for you to follow. But you are not making a holy manuscript. Do not spend tons of time getting the fonts, and the colors, and the bolding just right. That's not the point.

Lastly, do not cut-and-paste large swaths of text from your notes or from cases. Remember, outlining is a process. It requires you to think. By thinking you will learn the material and understand it better.

How to Outline

Drafting an outline takes several steps. Here are some basic suggestions for creating one.

A. Get Organized

Before you begin you will want to be organized. Ensure you're in a comfortable place with enough room to stretch out. At minimum, you should have with you: (1) the course syllabus; (2) the course casebook; (3) any course supplement, rule, or code book; (4) your class notes and case briefs; (5) any course materials or handouts; and (6) any supplementary resources you might have to help you understand the material (e.g., hornbooks). When crafting your outline, you will likely need to consult all these sources.

B. Organize Around Legal Topics

You want to begin by getting a sense of the big picture. You should organize your outline around concepts and legal topics, not around cases. In class you read cases. But the outline needs to be broader than that. It needs to focus on the main legal issues and principles of law that you studied. In your first year torts class, for example, you may have read hundreds of cases. Don't list those cases. Instead your torts outline should have headings that set out the main issues you studied, such as Negligence, Intentional Torts, Strict Liability, etc.

There's a fairly easy way to start an outline. Look at the main sections that you have covered in class from the table of contents or from the course's syllabus. Write them down. These will be the major sections of your outline. This will ensure that you are organizing your outline by topics and issues rather than by cases.

C. Subdivide into Legal Elements

After you have identified the main topics of the course from the table of contents, course syllabus, or from your class notes, you will subdivide the outline further. You should break each topic down into its main components, and include all the elements for each legal issue. Be sure to flesh out each part or sub-part with a definition or explanation.

When subdividing the main topics into components and legal elements, keep in mind the relationship between the sub-parts. Are they in the right order? Are they in the right hierarchy? Have you correctly identified the relationship between the rules and issues? For each rule or standard, you should break the rule or standard into elements and identify exceptions. From class you may have read many cases that discuss various elements of a larger rule. You should combine the teachings of those cases into one general rule.

For example, in Torts under a main topic of "Intentional Torts" you might have studied several different torts, such as assault, battery, false imprisonment, intentional infliction of emotional distress, etc. For each intentional tort, break out the tort by its elements.

D. Blend in Key Cases and Statutes

After you have identified the main topics, the key issues within each topic, and the elements to each legal issue, your next step is to include information about the relevant statutes, codes, or cases you studied. You should blend into your outline the important statutes or cases that relate to the sub-parts, as well as include hypotheticals or illustrations that demonstrate how the sub-parts or elements work.

Cases are examples of how the elements of a rule work in practice. In writing an exam answer, cases can be used as analogies. So be sure to note, very quickly, how the cases you have read demonstrate how the rule applies. When you come to the exam this exercise will allow you to make arguments by analogy (arguments that support a conclusion through comparing the facts of the problem with the facts of prior court decisions). On the other hand, be careful not to get bogged down in too many details. An outline should not be a compilation of case briefs.

E. Include Policy and Reasoning

For each rule, standard, test, or element, identify the policy behind it. Professors like to talk about policy. And in exams discussing policy can be the difference between an A and a B. Understanding the policy or reasons behind a particular rule will help you address tough questions in a nuanced, more sophisticated way. Why is the rule the way it is?

Your outline for intentional torts might look like this:

Intentional Torts

I. Assault
   A. The Elements:
      1. An act
      2. Intended to cause
      3. Apprehension of harmful or offensive conduct
   B. Key Cases & Statutory Provisions

C. Underlying Policy
D. An Example

Other Considerations

A few other things are worth keeping in mind as you begin outlining for a course.

A. The Condensed Outline

At some point, you should condense your outline to one or two pages. This should normally be done in the last few weeks before the exam, just as the course is ending. This very short outline serves as a checklist for the key points in the course. You will memorize this outline to ensure that you spot the issues being tested, and have a framework for attack.

You want to think of this as the step-by-step guide to the course and to answering an exam question. So usually the condensed outline is limited to the elements of the different legal rules you have studied. You should remove the cases and the examples that were contained in the longer outline. The longer outline helps you learn and synthesize the course material. The condensed outline is solely to give you something manageable to study while going into the exam.

B. It's a Personal Thing

Outlines can look very different. Don't worry if your outline is not as pretty as your friend's, or doesn't contain the exact same information. An outline is a tool that helps you understand and organize the material covered in class. What works for you, might not work for someone else. This is another reason why you want to create your own outline, rather than simply copy someone else's. While your outline must be complete, the length of an outline has little correlation to quality.

C. Flowcharts

Some students are visual learners. If you are, you might consider creating a flowchart for each course. Flowcharts are a different way of organizing the many rules you must learn, and understanding the relationship between those rules. Just like an outline, a flowchart can provide you with a plan of attack—a step-by-step approach—to analyzing a particular question. An outline may be more complicated than a flowchart and permits you to organize a large amount of material. Creating a flowchart forces you to think carefully about the different steps required in analyzing a particular area of law.

D. Open and Closed Book Exams

Some will tell you that an outline for a closed-book exam should look substantially different than an outline for an open-book exam (i.e., an exam where you may consult your notes and outline during the exam). Don't believe them. As a preliminary matter, whether you may bring an outline into the exam or not, the outline must be organized and structured in a way that you can synthesize and understand the material covered. An outline's primary purpose remains as a tool for learning the material, regardless of the style of exam given. More importantly, the "open" part of an open-book exam is often misleading. Usually even in an open book exam you must know the material by heart—you do not have time to consult your outline or notes.

There may be, however, some slight differences between how you outline for a closed-book exam as compared to an open-book exam. One difference may be the condensed outline. Generally a condensed outline, which contains just key concepts and rules, is more important for closed book exams where you must memorize the outline. Another difference may be the use of colors and tabs. In an open-book exam, some professors suggest coloring and tabbing your outline so that you can look things up more quickly during the exam (e.g., a different colored tab for each topic, and different colored ink for key rules).

That's it. That's how you will learn to take what is discussed in class and see how it al relates together. By outlining you will prepare for the final exam and will figure out the big picture yourself."

* * * * *

Cranky, yes. Not a pleasant dinner-companion, maybe. But Lawrence did have good advice. I was struggling to pull everything together. I was going to have to try what he suggested. Outlining sounded like a good idea.

The Basics

☐ Start the fourth or fifth week of the semester (first year)
☐ Create a schedule for updating outlines each week
☐ Write your outline as a roadmap for the final exam
☐ A study aid—worry about substance more than form

How to Do It

☐ Get ready (find a quiet place, bring course materials, notes etc.)
☐ Organize your outline around legal topics (not cases). Look at course syllabus or casebook table of contents for organizational ideas
☐ Subdivide each topic into their components
☐ Break each legal rule into its separate elements (write rule summaries)
☐ Blend in key cases and statutes around rules
☐ Include examples and hypos covered in class
☐ Note key policy considerations
☐ Keep it relatively short

Other Considerations

☐ Create a condensed outline near end of semester (just a few pages) with key rules

☐ Try working with flowcharts
☐ Tailor your outline depending on whether exam is open or closed book

Chapter 5

Studying

Musings of a cranky professor.... I like being a law professor. Each day is an adventure. That's the beauty of this job.

This morning I drive to school as I always do. My trusty 15-year old Ford puttering into my usual spot. I park and sit a second, bracing myself for the onslaught of the day ahead. I'm looking forward to class. We're covering some tough material. I could have some fun with my students. Didn't I make some big jock cry last year? That was an impressive bit of Socratic method! But no, I'm feeling generous. I'm in a good mood. Perhaps I'll lecture a little. Maybe I'll even try to help them with some studying tips. No need to be too hard on the kiddies, I think. I'm feeling in fine form and the thought of class brings a hint of a smile to my face. And with those thoughts, I open the car door.

Reality, however, is not so kind. As I get out of my car, I hear a friendly "Good morning." I look up. Right next to me is a young guy. I squint at him. He looks familiar. Vaguely though. Name? I'm at a loss. Perhaps a student from last year's course. "Uh, yeah." I mutter back something else unintelligible. As a professor, you always have to be friendly to your students—my Dean tells me it's part of the job. Hopefully this isn't one of those students who likes to talk. I don't have time to be chummy. Class starts soon. I close my car door and turn around.

And that's when I see what he's standing next to: a Mercedes. It's a sedan—a big, shiny one. Looks brand new. I can almost smell the leather seats from where I'm standing. A Mercedes. Now, what's wrong with this picture? Here I am, in my more advanced years and an accomplished (okay, tolerated) chaired professor, with a BA, JD, MA, Ph.D.—and here's this young buck

—almost a teenager (yes, he can't be too old, I see pimples)—driving a $150,000 car. And he's not alone. There next to it is a new BMW, and what's that, a Bentley!? You've got to be kidding me. If you can afford a Bentley, you shouldn't be a law student. Sell it and retire for goodness sake. I look at my Ford. It's a little dented and the paint is peeling. It's seen better days. Pitiful. Life's not fair.

He's still looking at me with that warm, friendly smile plastered on his face. Infuriating. I don't know why, but I feel like I should just reach out, grab him, and slap him silly. Knock that grin right off his face. That would be gutsy, inspiring even. It might take the edge off. My colleagues later, of course, would all shake their heads as I'm hauled off to the loony-bin—"Such a shame about Lawrence losing it like that. The old coot. Oh well, at least they'll give him a padded room." But secretly and very quietly, they'd be singing my praises, admiring my chutzpa ("about time, serves the student right"). I return to reality. I constrain myself. Violence averted, at least for now.

Mercedes-boy is still looking at me. He locks his car, nods his head, gives me one last smile and an affable wave. "Well, see you at the faculty meeting," he says. He heads to the faculty building. Uh. Oh. Well, so much for that. Not a student at all. Now I recognize him. Our new faculty hire. Impressive resume, if I remember right. Closer to his mid-forties than his twenties. Clerked for the U.S. Supreme Court, or something like that. Made a name for himself at some big-name Wall Street firm. Oops. Must remember to get my eyes checked.

Well, time for class. I'm getting old. I guess I'll tell my students how to study.

———

"Preparing for class means more than pulling the facts and holding from a case. It means more than giving the cases a quick read. You are in law school to learn how to analyze, to question the reasoning in the opinions, and exercise your own judgment about them. It is hard work and there is no easy way around it.

Before Class

In preparing for class, remembering the purpose of law school is essential. You are not here just to learn the law. You are here to learn to analyze critically and to think creatively. You must think beyond the facts at hand, to work through issues presented by cases and exercise your own judgment about them. That requires careful preparation and study.

A. Setting a Schedule

Ensuring adequate preparation time for each and every class will require setting a study schedule and sticking with it. You will create a schedule. You will stick with it.

You will schedule three hours of study time for every hour of class. I do not mean three hours a week for each class you have. I mean three hours each week for every hour you are in class. If you meet for twelve hours during the week, you will schedule approximately thirty six hours of studying time for the week. (What, you say—that's more than forty hours a week? Heaven forbid. Welcome to real life kiddo!)

During the scheduled study time, you will read and brief cases, prepare for class, prepare your own outlines, review your outlines, and take practice exams. During the first few weeks of law school, just reading and briefing cases will absorb most of your study time. By around the fourth week, it will be time to begin outlining. Reviewing outlines, making flashcards, and taking practice exams will start soon thereafter. Studying for exams cannot wait until finals week. It must be part of your weekly routine.

As I mentioned in an earlier lecture, some of you will prepare for class during the week (the night before each class) and save the weekend hours for outlining, reviewing, and taking practice exams. Others will finish the entire week's reading over the weekend so you can spend each night after class updating your outlines and taking practice exams. Both strategies are fine. Your approach may vary, but you will allocate your time between all of these areas and you will not wait until dead week to start preparing for exams.

You will be tempted to put work off until the end of the semester. It won't work. This isn't college. Once your schedule is
made, you must stay with it. Socializing with your friends does not
count toward your schedule study time each week—even if you
are talking about torts while at the local pub.

B. The Right Environment

When studying, ensure you are in a comfortable place without
distractions. Ideally you should be in a place where you have
enough room to stretch out. Before beginning, think ahead so you
have what you need for the next hour. You don't want to be jumping up every few minutes to get a book, or a pen, or another cup
of coffee.

C. Before Reading a Case

Often there is an introduction to the case that you may have a
hankering to skip. Don't. The introduction will place the case in context and will often indicate the statute or constitutional provision on
which the court bases its decision. If the casebook tells you to read
Article III of the Constitution or read a Federal Rule of Civil Procedure before reading the case, you will look it up and read it carefully.
If you don't, you likely will understand the case only superficially. If
you have a "rule book" or a "statutory supplement" for a course, it
should be tired, well-worn and dog-eared by the semester's end.

D. Reading a Case

We have talked previously about how to read a case to write a
case brief. But preparing properly involves more than creating a
brief. Certainly you need to know the facts, holding and reasoning of the case. But you need to know more than that. You need
to understand the case well enough so that you are prepared to answer questions I will ask in class.

After you've read a case you should understand it at a sophisticated level. You should be able to tell me how the decision directly

affects the two parties involved. You should have an opinion on whether the court applied the law correctly; whether the majority or the dissent have the more powerful argument; whether the case is consistent with cases previously discussed or consistent with other cases assigned for the day's reading. You should know which of the facts are most important and how the court's holding would change if you took one fact away. What is the slightest factual change that would lead to a different outcome? You should know why we are reading the case in this section of the chapter, rather than another. You should have an opinion on whether the court correctly applied precedent and, if not, why. Was precedent ignored because the judge believed justice required one party to prevail over another? Did public policy sway the court's decision? Only when you have done this for all of your assigned cases will you be "prepared for class."

E. Don't Forget the Book Notes

In preparing for class, you will read not only the cases assigned, but the notes that follow. For most casebooks, although not all, following a case will be a series of numbered paragraphs (called notes) that provide additional information about the case or the topic being studied, and usually ask questions of the reader.

Professors will often assign the notes as part of your reading. Even if the notes are not part of your assigned reading, you should read them because they provide guidance in analyzing the case and can assist you in figuring out how the case fits into the chapter. For some casebooks, the only way to understand a heavily edited case is to read the notes. Read the notes and think about the questions asked. If a note tells you to look something up, look it up.

F. Immediately Before Class

Arrive early to class. You should arrive approximately fifteen minutes early to review your notes and prepare for class. As you should have already caught on to, I start every class by reviewing what we previously discussed. Nothing infuriates me more than a student who cannot repeat back to me what we learned the class before. It makes me think you weren't listening. That offends me.

Expect that I will start the class by reviewing what we have already covered. That practice, although not universal, is fairly common among law professors. Right before class, go back and look at your notes from the day before. Familiarize yourself with the points we covered so when asked a question you can respond. Then move on to reviewing the cases that were assigned for that day's class. Remind yourself of the facts, issues, and holdings of the cases. Think about how the new cases fit in to what we already discussed. Anticipate what I will cover in the next lecture. Anticipate what questions I will ask.

During Class

Part of studying effectively depends on what you do in class. During class you will take selective notes, listen carefully to your classmates, and avoid being overly reliant on your laptop.

A. Listen Carefully

An obvious point: you must listen carefully. Sit up and pay attention. Sit in a place in class where it's easy for you to see the professor and stay alert. Make sure you've slept enough so you don't nod off or daydream. If you can't hear what I'm saying (or your other professors) move closer to the front of the classroom. If your professors speak too quietly, ask them to speak up. If you can't hear my bellowing, get a hearing aid.

B. Take Selective Notes

Law school is not like college. You must not write down everything said in class. You will feel pressure to. You may want to. But you should not. If you write everything down, your chances of failure increase. The best students take selective notes. How many notes? Not many at all. The worst students write down everything.

I will let you in on a little secret law professors have. Here it is: professors rarely say more than one or two important things in an hour class. Most of what they say is useless. For me, you should feel fortunate if I make one relevant point each week. Normally, I ramble. I spend most of the time talking to myself. And if I forget to take my meds, watch out! So if you write down everything I spew, you are writing down meaningless garbage. And when, weeks later, you return to your notes, you will find gobbledygook. If you take selective notes, they will be a resource for studying. If you write down everything, you will be lost in piles of paper with disorganized, useless information. If you do that, good luck. Life around exam time is going to be painful.

You want my cranky opinion? Taking too many notes reflects laziness. Writing down everything I say is easy. To be discriminating is difficult. By writing everything down, you distract yourself from the real point of class—thinking about the material. Write legibly. Write only key points. What is the rule? What is the policy? What is the key reasoning? What is the professor's opinion? That's what your notes should reflect.

Now, don't misunderstand me. Students who show up to class without pen and paper are dunderheads. You must take *some* notes. Notes are important. By writing notes and then working with those notes immediately after class, you retain and learn the material better. Notes are critical for later preparing for exams. By taking notes, you can keep track of items you do not understand, material you need to read, and important points your professor has emphasized. But your notes should be succinct, short, and easily understood. Figure that balance out and you will get much more out of law school.

More important than taking notes is what you do with them. Immediately after class, you will look over your notes. It will take about ten minutes. Do not get up. Do not chat with friends. Stay right where you are, in your seat. This is critical. Right after class, you must review your notes. Jot down the two or three key points from the lecture. Highlight important things. Make your notes more legible. Review. This is the time to ensure that you understood what the class was all about.

A final point on this. I am a luddite. You won't catch me using PowerPoint, or any of those fancy computer thing-a-ma-bobs. But many professors will (fools that they are). If your professor uses PowerPoint, please, for the love of God, do not copy down everything from every slide. That is asinine. Ask your professor to provide you with a copy of the slides after class. Sure, copying down everything may help you improve your typing speed. It will not help you be a lawyer. Lawyers do not transcribe. If you want to transcribe, become a court reporter. Court reporters usually make more money anyway.

C. Take Consistent and Organized Notes

Not only should your notes be selective, your notes should be consistent in style and format, and they should be organized. Consider including a heading for the first page of every day of notes (e.g., date, topic, etc.). Some students take notes in an outline format, others use mind-mapping software, others use a note-taking software. Whatever you choose, be certain to be consistent. After a semester, you may have a hundred of pages of notes for a course. Organizing the notes as you write will make the notes more useful when you later review.

One important caveat: whatever format or style you choose, it should be simple and straightforward. If the format becomes too elaborate, note-taking will focus your efforts away from what the law professor is saying. You do not want to be distracted with mind-numbing details such as whether you should create a subheading or a sub-sub heading, or whether that particular note should be in green, blue, or red. Contrary to what some students believe, having Technicolor notes may well be counter-productive (certainly, if your notes look like a J-Crew catalogue—with case names in bright rhubarb, facts in deep aubergine, rules in heather ice, holdings in light parsley, and policy in Nantucket fog—you've gone too far).

D. Listen to Your Classmates

You may feel that most of my class is spent with your classmates' amateur and unsophisticated attempts to analyze what the law is or should be. Some of your fellow students, bored by these interchanges, will be lured into playing solitaire or instant messaging their best friend. You will resist these temptations. You will listen to what your classmates are saying.

Why? Because by listening to your classmates you learn how to discern between good and bad arguments. Class time is meant to enhance your analytical skills. On an exam you will include only strong arguments. The process of listening to your classmates will help train you to do that.

By listening to your classmates, you will also better understand my response to their answers. And in doing so you will start to develop an understanding of what my expectations are for the exam. I will rarely tell you an answer. Rather, you will need to develop a sense of how I want you to approach the law based on listening to the questions I ask and whether I like your classmate's answer.

Do not spend class time getting ready for the next case. You may think it's wise to use the time I am asking your friend a question to review for the next case in the chance I call on you. This is another form of distraction. You will not become distracted. When I ask a question of one of your classmates, you should attempt to answer the question quietly yourself, and then evaluate how your answer compares to your classmate's. Be sure you understand the legal issues being discussed so you know if you have any questions that you need to ask.

Ultimately, if you don't stay focused on the discussion, when I call on you it will not matter whether you were Googling on your laptop or studying for the next case—you will not have heard the question and will be forced to ask "Can you repeat the question?" Which is really just another way of saying "Sorry Professor, I haven't been listening!" Of course, when I respond "Not a problem. I'm happy to repeat the question," I really mean "Little snot. Waste my time will you—I'll show you. I'll get you with my final exam."

E. Use Your Laptop Appropriately

If you are one of my laptop users, you may be enticed to go online during class. Have will power. Do not go online unless instructed to do so. Do not instant message your friends. Do not play solitaire. Misuse of your laptop will cause you to miss important information. You may notice that person next to you who is looking at her "MySpace" page always responds with "Can you repeat the question?" You know how I feel about that response.

Don't go online. If you can't resist the temptation, leave your laptop at home. Take written notes. You will learn more that way. Not only will you be less distracted by having a computer in front of you, but you will be forced to be more discerning about what notes to take and therefore more engaged in class.

After Class

How you approach studying after class is equally important as how you approach studying to prepare for class.

A. As Class Ends

After class review is as important, if not more important, than preparing before class. Spend ten minutes after each class reviewing what you covered in class, and writing down the key points your professor emphasized. Were your case briefs complete? How did this material relate to other material that you've covered in other classes? What new rules did you learn? Spending just a few minutes after class ensures that you understand the material, and gives you an opportunity to identify any lingering questions you may have on a topic, while the topic is fresh in your mind. If something is unclear, now is the time to discuss with your study group or with the professor.

B. Use Your Professor Effectively

One of the most valuable and under-used resources in law school are your professors. Many of you will go to the book store and load up on horn books, commercial outlines, case summaries, varies supplements, review books, and exam prep materials. Yet you will fail to avail yourselves of the number one learning support opportunity—talking one on one with me.

Visiting me in office hours is essential. Not only will you get your questions answered, but you will begin to establish a relationship. Developing a professional, personal relationship with your professor can be one of the more rewarding aspects of law school and a powerful strategy for future success. A majority of your professors will be experts in their field. They may have practiced and will be able to give you advice about your career. They will also be in the position to write you the strongest letters of recommendation and serve as references and contacts for future employment opportunities. Don't walk into my office and ask me for a letter of recommendation after introducing yourself for the first time. I only write letters for those I know.

If a professional relationship is not a sufficient motivation to visit your professor, then go to office hours to help improve your preparation for the final exam. Who better to ask about what is expected on the exam than the one writing the exam? You will discover a lot about my expectations and style just by talking with me during office hours. Like many professors, I will grade a practice exam for you and I will be happy to discuss the results of the exam in office hours. These discussions can lead to invaluable insight into the depth of analysis and organization I expect of my students.

Regardless of this advice, many of you will not take advantage of opportunity to visit me during office hours. Some of you will feel you have no questions, so you will assume you do not need to see me. Others, who are struggling, may be too embarrassed to ask me a question. Still others will assume I am too busy to be bothered with student questions.

Ignore these feelings as they surface throughout the semester. If you don't have a question, identify a legal issue that came up in class that you would like to discuss further. If you are embarrassed or worried about intruding—get over it! Keep in mind that professors genuinely enjoy helping students. It is the part of the job that we love. We sit through committee meetings, perform inane administrative tasks, grade endless amounts of exams, all so we can do what we love, teaching! You coming to me for help may turn out to be the highlight of my day because I actually was able to teach—which is why I got into the job in the first place.

C. Limits on Using Your Professor

Although building a relationship with me (and your other professors) is important, a line exists between appropriate and inappropriate contact with your professor. Unless you are struggling and need special assistance, a visit once or twice a month is sufficient. Stalking your professor is not the type of relationship you want to build.

A note on e-mail—in today's society, sometimes it seems easier to simply shoot off an e-mail rather than go into office hours. This is appropriate when your question is discrete and requires a short response. Any question that involves a complex discussion of legal issues should be addressed during office hours. For me, don't bother with e-mail. I don't have e-mail. I don't check e-mail. I don't respond to e-mail. You may feel free to write me using quill and parchment. If your calligraphy is acceptable, I may write a response.

D. Using Study Groups Effectively

For those of you who base your expectations of law school on what you have seen in movies like *Legally Blonde*, study groups may seem like the end-all, be-all of the law school experience. Relying on study groups however, if they become your primary method of studying, can be detrimental to your law school career. Study groups should play a useful, but probably a limited, role in your study regime.

Study groups are helpful because they allow you to talk out ideas which can be helpful in developing your analytical skills. Reviewing class materials with others will point out any holes in your outlines and allow you to find out if you missed a concept or definition that is important to know. Study groups provide a forum for you to quiz each other, will allow you to share studying techniques, and will present you with different perspectives or approaches to the law that you had not thought of before.

There are different approaches to study groups. A study group may meet on a weekly basis to go over what was covered in class that week. A study group might get together only at the end of the semester to prepare for finals. Other groups meet each morning as a way to prepare for class. No matter what approach a study group takes, it should not be the primary source of studying. To be effective, all the students in group must be committed to the group and contribute.

Choose your study group partners carefully. Your best friend, the funniest person in the class, the best looking of your classmates may not be the best choice of study partners. This is not high school. Your goal is not to be in the cool kids' group. You're not trolling for a spouse either. For you to get the most out of your study group, you need study partners who are also willing to do the work before they get to the group. You need people who are focused on studying not socializing.

Keeping your study group to a small number is often wise— perhaps three or four students. Study groups with too many students become inefficient. For the group to be effective, each member of the group must have time to participate and talk. And generally, you should agree on some ground rules before the group begins. What is the goal or objective of the group? What happens if a member fails to show? What if a member is habitually late? How will the group resolve conflicts? Figuring out these things ahead of time will save time in the long run and ensure a more productive group.

A good use of a study group is to take practice exams. The group can take an exam under timed conditions and then exchange answers so that other members of the group can critique them.

E. Avoid Study Group Don'ts

A few "don'ts" with study groups. Do not join a study group to socialize and meet your future spouse. Do not join a study group to lessen the work load. Do not divide courses and assign each person an outline to do. This is one of the dangers of study groups and a mistake. The point of creating outlines is the learning process. Outlining allows you to organize your notes and thoughts in a way that the material makes logical sense. You are preparing for exams as you are outlining. By relying on someone else's outline you run the risk of missing important concepts: trying to study from someone else's outline is an exercise in futility.

A study group should be used to review concepts discussed in class and as a sounding board for ideas. If you join a study group in which the members want to divide the work, this is an indicator that you have a group of people who are looking for the easy road. Find a new group. If your study group routinely meets in a bar, where more drinking is done than studying, this is also an indicator that it is time to find a new group.

F. As the Semester Ends

As the semester nears the end, your studying should focus less on preparing for class, and more on getting ready to take final exams. Be sure to study each subject separately. Don't fall into the trap of studying too extensively for one course and too little for others.

In the last four-to-five weeks of the semester, spend most of your time learning actively. Passive learning involves reading and reviewing outlines. Active learning includes finishing your outlining, writing up flashcards, and taking practice exams. You want to use the materials you are studying.

You'll be busy. As the semester ends you can expect to be working 10–12 hours a day (including class time).

* * * * *

That was helpful. Here are my notes for the lecture.

The Basics

☐ Create a study schedule (three hours of study for each hour of class)

☐ Study in a quiet, distraction-free place

☐ Read all assigned cases carefully (don't forget the notes!)

☐ Immediately before class review notes, cases and briefs

☐ Immediately after class review class notes (what were the key points?)

☐ Study actively (write and create, and take practice exams, don't just review)

☐ Study a lot! Law school is like a full-time job

During Class

☐ Engage and listen carefully

☐ Take selective notes

☐ Disable internet (no surfing or e-mail)

☐ Take consistent, organized notes in a straightforward format

☐ Pay attention to classmates when they are asked questions (what is the professor focusing on?)

Notes on Study Groups

☐ Choose group carefully

☐ Keep small (perhaps three or four students)

☐ Agree on group expectations and goals

☐ Set study group ground rules

☐ Set time to meet (and keep to it)

☐ Stay focused during study group meetings (not the time to socialize!)

☐ Don't divide up outlines

☐ Don't meet in pubs and bars (damn! is there no fun in law school...)

Chapter 6

Final Exams

Musings of a cranky professor.... It's Friday night and the clock strikes 8 p.m. I stare across my oak desk in my study brandishing my weapons of choice: a fountain pen in my right hand, a tumbler with a healthy dose of scotch in my left. My adversary—a formidable stack of exams—is across the desk, mocking me. Exams. The worst part of my job. Frankly, exam grading is depressing. I thought I had taught my students something when, suddenly, I realize some of them learned nothing. If only I could put it off another day.

But now I have no choice. I can't put it off. Across the study the red light on my answering machine is blinking. I don't need to listen to the messages. I know what they say. The Associate Dean has been calling on and off all week. I'm late with my exams. Actually, several weeks late. He's threatened to fine me in various ways. Hah, let the pipsqueak try. But after procrastinating for weeks, even I'm starting to feel guilty. I am out of options. I can't stall any longer. I have to begin.

I take a sip of scotch and rip open the first exam and turn to the first page. "What, for heavens sake. Pink!" I gawp. "Why? For what possible reason?!" Yet I confirm it. The entire exam is written in pink ink. What next? Crayon? Ridiculous. What does the student think this is, cheerleading camp? With a flourish, I write the letters F-A-I-L in large cursive over the page. Wait. I pause. It's not quite right. I put a little heart over the "i" and finish it with an exclamation point. I smile. Perfect. Even poetic. That will teach the poor chump. I look up. It's 8:01 p.m. Mmm. Not bad. One down, eighty or so more to go. Perhaps exam grading isn't so bad after all. At this rate, I'll be done in no time. I take another sip of scotch bracing myself.

I open the next exam. This one I read for awhile until I toss it aside, revolted. It's one of those exams where the student has gone to great lengths to disguise the fact he knows nothing. Oh, it's a clever ploy. I'll give him that. He starts by restating every fact of the exam question, as if I'm a moron who can't remember what I wrote. This student is particularly adept at repeating the rules *ad nauseam*, perhaps hoping that I don't recognize he has nothing meaningful to say. And then he rambles on about everything under the sun for pages and pages, everything that is except for the issues the exam raises. It's as if the student has been desperately holding in every tidbit of information that was discussed in the semester, no matter how tangential. Intellectually constipated, so to speak. And then, unable to contain it any longer, he's disgorged the whole nasty mess on the page.

After wallowing through pages of this absolute drivel, written with the grammatical adroitness of a 2-year-old, I'm feeling nauseous myself. It's the ending though that's absolutely brilliant. Instead of answering the question asked, the student for some inexplicable reason goes wild, wailing on and on about justice, God, country, the evils of Capitalism, and how the children are the future. Any semblance of common sense or judgment has been completely tossed as he waxes on. I like a good policy discussion, but this blighter is obviously more than a little soft in the head. I dribble a few drops of ink from my fountain pen on some random pages (I need to give the appearance that I labored over the exam). I then scrawl "C+" across the first page—the plus because I'm feeling somewhat grateful the exam wasn't written in pink.

I take another swig of scotch. Perhaps three's the charm, I think, as I tear open the next exam. If only I was so lucky. My exam question had been straightforward. A clear call of the question, centered at the bottom of the page: "Should the court grant the motion to dismiss?" And then next to it, in bold: "The court has jurisdiction. Do *not* discuss any jurisdictional issues." So how does this student's exam begin? "The first issue is whether the court has jurisdiction." I'm stunned. Completely baffled. It then proceeds for two full pages to set out elaborate jurisdictional rules, only to conclude: "But as the exam says, the court has jurisdiction so no further analysis is needed." Lord have mercy. This is painful. I can't resist. I write in almost manic cursive on the side of the page: "What the frak were you thinking!!! Read the question. I told you not to discuss jurisdiction." I pitch this third exam to my growing pile of misfit answers, disgusted.

I say though, I like the word *frak*. It has a nice ring to it. My 22-year-old granddaughter taught it to me last year. She's a smart one that girl. Sharp as a whip. Apparently it's the invention of some TV show—Star Wars, Flash Gordon, Battlestar Gigactica, or something or another. I can't remember. But I like it. I like to write *frak*, or maybe *freakin*, a few times a semester on exams. It's guaranteed to get back to the Dean at some point. I chuckle. I can see him now, staring blankly for a moment in a ghastly sort of way as he tries to explain that one to some angry parent. Aah, the beauty of tenure.... Perhaps life isn't so bad. The glass is half-full after all!

The mention of a glass brings me back to a more pressing reality, and I look at my tumbler. Not half-full at all. Not even quarter-full. Not even a drop. Just plain empty. Damn. How could I have let this happen. Although, I wonder—perhaps this much scotch and exams don't mix so well together. Oh well, at least a sip of the good stuff now and then gives me something else to focus on than my own suffering. I can't believe it. Only three done. Another eighty or so more to go. I'm getting old. Perhaps I should just throw them down the stairs like I did last year.

I let out a tiny sigh. It's going to be a long night. Tomorrow in class I'll tell my students how they should prepare and write an essay exam....

Before the Exam

To do well in law school you must do well on your final exams. Law school is different from many graduate programs. Usually for first-year courses, students will take one exam at the end of the semester or year worth 100% of the grade. It doesn't matter how brilliant you were in class, or whether you understood the subtleties of the law, or whether you are beloved by your professor. If you don't do well on the final exam, you've got nothing.

My essay exams—like most first-year essay exams—follow a standard format: they set out a complex fact pattern, pose a hypothetical legal problem, and then ask you to resolve that problem. To do well, you must: (1) spot the relevant legal issues; (2) identify the legal principles or rules applicable to those issues; (3) identify the key facts upon which each issue turns; and (4) draw a conclusion in a logical, analytical way. Rarely in my exams will one "right" answer exist. This will be true for most of your professor's exams. Your conclusion is much less important than your analysis and how you reach the conclusion.

Law school exams are also not like college exams. In your undergraduate classes if you parroted back the information you read, you would do fine. You might even do very well. Not so in law school. For law school exams, you must apply the legal principles you have learned to a new factual context. Merely spitting back rules that you have memorized is worth little. Writing everything you know about the course will lead to failure. You have to do more. You must write a clear, concise, and thoughtful answer to the legal question posed.

This all too abstract? Okay. Here are some specific guidelines for getting prepared for your final exams. Follow them. Don't improvise.

A. Know Your Professor

You are not just writing an exam; you are writing an exam for a specific professor. This is important. Each professor has their own quirks and requirements. To do well, you must have a sense of how your professor will test you and how the professor will grade the exam. Will the exam be open book? Closed book? Take-home? Does the professor use essay questions, multiple choice, something else? What is the professor looking for in an answer?

The best way to figure out how a professor will test is to look at their prior exams. Prynceton Law, like many schools, requires that I either post my exams online, or hold them on reserve in the school's library. I have been teaching since the Mesozoic Era, so you've got plenty to look at. You should look at a course's past exams early on in the semester. Within the first few weeks of the course, you want a sense of how the professor will evaluate you so that you may tailor your studying and preparation.

B. Keep Your Outline Updated

Daily preparation matters. You will not do well in law school if you cram all your studying into the final weeks of the term. Keeping your course outline up to date is critical. Each week, you should review the material you've learned from the prior week and place it in your outline. Keeping your outline updated is also a good way of seeing how different cases covered in class fit into the larger topics you are studying. Your outline is your primary study tool for the final exam—don't forget it.

C. Schedule Practice Exams

Do not wait until the end of the semester or until you have completed your outline to start taking practice exams. One of the biggest mistakes a student can make is to wait to take practice exams until after they have finished all their studying, outlines, and briefs. You want to start taking practice exams early in the semester.

Practicing is the best way to improve and to learn the law, so reserve specific time to practice. At the start of the semester set up a schedule to ensure that you will have time set aside to take sufficient practice exams. Perhaps starting in the fourth week of the semester, you should take as many as two timed, practice essay exams each week. Generally this will mean that you will take a practice exam in a particular subject once every two weeks. One study in the mid-1990s showed that students who took practice exams in their first-semester of law school on average substantially raised their GPAs.

Ideally, you should take six or more practice one-hour essay exams for each course that you are enrolled in. Since law school exams are generally different from other sorts of tests that students have previously encountered, students who write out practice exams are less likely to be shocked when they face their first real exam. If any of your professors use multiple-choice tests, you should also answer hundreds of practice multiple-choice questions before the actual exam.

Usually, your professor will make past exams available. If your professor does, take advantage of it. Your own professor's exams are the best place to turn to first. If your professor, however, does not have past exams, you can easily find samples. There's plenty of sample first-year exams on the internet, and most libraries will carry commercial exam preparation guides. But ideally you want to practice exams that are similar to your professor's style and format.

When taking a practice exam, follow a three-step process.

1. *Timed Practice*: First take the exam timed, under conditions as closely mimicking the actual exam experience as possible. If you are taking a one-hour practice essay exam, you should set aside approximately three hours to work on the exam. If your final exam will be closed book (i.e., no notes), your practice exam should also be closed book. If your final exam will be open book, your practice exam should be open book. Do not worry if early in the semester you find it difficult to answer the question.

2. *Open Book Review*: After the allocated time is over, go back to your answer and using your notes, outline, casebook, or other materials see what parts of the exam you would change. Could your answer be better organized? Have you used clear headings and subheadings to separate the different issues in the analysis? Is your analysis as developed as you would have liked? Have you accurately stated the law? In this second stage you are using the exam to learn the law and seek out answers to particular questions.

3. *Self-Assessment*: Lastly, in step three, look at the model answer (if you have one) and assess how well you did. Is the exam well-organized? Did you spot the correct issues? How close is your answer to the model answer? Did you use all the facts of the question in your answer? Depending on how well you answered the question, this may be the time to visit you professor during office hours.

D. Approach Practice Exams Effectively

Whether you follow the above recommendations, be sure to take some practice exams under timed conditions. You can always revisit the exam afterwards to study the legal issues the exam raises more thoroughly. But the benefit is that you get to experience the practice exam under similar conditions as your final exam. By taking timed practice exams, you will hone your test-taking skills. This includes honing your ability to: (1) allocate your time, (2) identify areas of law that you don't understand; (3) spot issues; and (4) work under pressure. Most exams are time-pressured. So taking an exam under timed conditions is critical to doing well.

E. Learn How Your Professor Grades

Remember, you are not just taking an exam, you are taking "my exam." Not only do you want to know what my exams look like, you want to know how I grade. Some professors spend hours closely scrutinizing exams; others read them very quickly. Some use a point system that awards you credit for the mere mention of an argument, while others focus more on how skillfully you make the argument. Some take points off for incorrect answers, others only award points for correct answers. Some award points for creative, push-the-boundary type arguments, while some professors award no points for them. Some professors care about how well you write, while others are not concerned about writing style, grammar, or punctuation at all. Find out what your professor cares about, and make sure you meet those expectations. If your professors offer to review your written work and provide feedback, take them up on their offers. You'd be foolish not to.

F. Go to Review Sessions

For many courses, professors will hold exam workshops or review sessions. Sometimes professors teach these sessions, other times they are taught by teaching assistants. If your professor holds an exam workshop, attendance is not optional (no matter what the professor says). Be sure to attend. Often professors will consciously, or subconsciously, give exam tips during the review sessions. Review sessions are a good way to get insight into what your particular professor is looking for in an answer. The same is true if professors use teaching assistants. Meeting with teaching assistants is often a means to get information about the professor, how the professor grades, and what is most likely to be tested on the exam.

A related point. Most schools these days have very sophisticated academic support programs or offices. Experts on learning and law school teach and direct these programs. Often schools will have student mentors, writing centers, exam workshops, and a variety of other support programs. Look for these resources and use them. Many students don't use these resource. You will. You're not playing with a full deck if you ignore them.

G. Know the Legal Rules Cold

Knowing the law (i.e., the legal rules) that you have studied during the semester is a prerequisite to doing well. Knowing the law won't guarantee you a good grade. But not knowing the law will guarantee a poor grade, and possibly a failing one.

You have to know the rules down cold. A final exam is time-pressured. You will not have time to think through or look up the relevant law (even if it's an open-book, open-notes exam). Instead, you have to be comfortable enough with the law that once you spot an issue, you can quickly set out the legal standard, test, or factors that determine how the legal issue should be resolved.

This doesn't mean that you should mindlessly memorize legal rules. Dunderheads memorize. Lawyers do something more. Simple memorization is the wrong emphasis. Instead, you will know the rules by heart because you have seen them in the cases you read, included them in your case briefs, reviewed them before class, discussed them in class, studied them after class and in study groups, included them in your outline, and used them when writing practice exams.

H. No All-Nighters and Manage Stress

Law school exams require you to think and be on your game. If you stay up all night studying in the days leading up to an exam, you will be tired. If you're tired, you won't be able to focus. And if you are not able to give the exam the focus you need, you will do poorly. More importantly, you'll be wiped out for the next exam. Because many students take three to five exams over an approximate two-week exam period, pulling all-nighters is a recipe for disaster. You must get a good night's sleep before the exam.

During the exam period, you should eat well, and get enough sleep and exercise. This is critical. Managing stress and staying healthy is as important to doing well as how you study.

I. Typing v. Handwriting

One of the decisions students usually must make is whether to handwrite or type their final exams. The majority of law students type their exams on laptop computers. Most law schools permit this, requiring that students use an exam software that restricts access to a limited word processing program. Because most students will take the bar exam using a laptop computer, it's generally recommended that students type their law school exams too.

For my class you will type, and if you're smart you'll type all your exams. Professors prefer type-written exams because they are easier to read and therefore easier to grade. When I was young, students took pride in their penmanship. Now all I see is chicken-scratch. I don't like chicken-scratch and neither do my colleagues. Some recent studies have found that students who type their law school essay examinations perform better than students who handwrite. Ineligible handwriting will near guarantee a poor grade. If you do handwrite, use blue or black ink. Save your pinks, reds, and purples for writing love sonnets, or whatever else you kids write these days.

Starting the Exam

So what you should you do on the day of the exam and at the very start of the exam?

A. Arrive Early

You have enough things to worry about, don't add additional stress by arriving late to the exam. Arrive 20–30 minutes early (some schools require that you arrive even earlier if you are typing your exams). Be also sure that you know where your exam will be given, or give yourself plenty of time to find the exam room. Arriving early will also allow you to select a good place to sit during the exam. Select a spot to take the test that enables you to have enough space to work. Do not go to an exam on an empty stomach. Be sure to eat before going to an exam (drinking five cups of coffee and pounding cans of Red Bull is not eating).

B. Arrive Prepared

An obvious point: be sure you arrive prepared, with sufficient pens, pencils, and highlighters, or whatever else you plan to use on the exam. If you are typing your exam, ensure that your laptop is working properly and that any exam-taking software the school requires is working well.

You also should dress comfortably, and be ready for different room conditions (think layers, so that you can adapt to excessive air-conditioners, broken heaters, and the like). Many schools will permit you to bring a silent, non-digital (analog) timer to the exam, calculators, earplugs, and even snacks. Figure out before hand what your school permits, and come prepared.

Right before the exam is not the time to start cramming. Relax. You've studied hard. You will do fine. Nothing in the last few minutes before the exam will change how you will do, and may unnecessarily add to the stress. Never jump into a last-minute panic conversation with your classmates about course topics in the few minutes leading up to the exam.

C. Read the Instructions

The first thing you should do is read the instructions carefully, and then follow them. If the exam says, "write a memo"—you will write a memo. If the exam says, assume a certain fact—you will assume that fact. If an exam says, do not address an issue—you will not address that issue. If the exam tells you to play a role (e.g., to write a bench memo as a judge's clerk, or serve as the attorney for the defendant), then be sure to play that role. It doesn't matter what the instructions say, you will follow them. If I tell you to put little hearts above your "i"s, you will write little hearts above your "i"s.

Reading the instructions carefully sounds like common sense. But every year students forget. You will not. Some of the most unfortunate exam mistakes (i.e., not answering the question asked, running out of time, or focusing on incorrect issues) can be traced to the student's failure to carefully read the exam instructions.

D. Allocate Your Time

After carefully reading the instructions, you should flip through the exam and allocate the time you intend to spend on each section of the exam. You should also allocate how much time you can spend on each question within an exam section.

This is important. If the exam tells you how much time to spend on each question, then do exactly what the exam tells you. If the exam does not specify, then allocate your time based on the relative worth of the exam question. If you have a two-hour exam, with two essay questions, you will spend one hour on each essay. If it's a two-hour exam, and one essay is worth 60% and the other 40%, then you will spend 72 minutes on the first question, and 48 minutes on the second (I know, crazy math, but you'll figure it out). Once you have allocated your time, you will follow it strictly. If you allocate an hour to the first essay and the hour is up—you must move on.

Do not fall into the trap of spending all your time on one question. Many students when starting law school make this mistake.

You must answer every question asked in the exam to do well. An "A" grade on the first essay, and an "F" grade on the second essay —it still a C grade. An amazing answer on the first question, will never make up for the last question you did not answer. Allocate your time and stick with it. Once your time is up for one part of the exam you will stop and you will move on.

E. Read the Call of the Question

For most essay exams, the professor will have a "call of the question"—sometimes referred to as an interrogatory—at the end of a fact pattern. The "call," will tell you what the professor wants you to do. After you have allocated your time, you should turn to the first essay question and read the call of that essay question carefully. Read the call of the question before you read the fact pattern. This way when you read the fact pattern you should more easily be able to spot the significance of certain facts.

This related point seems too basic, but it is one of the most common mistakes students make: answer the question that your professors asks. I do not want an essay on everything we discussed in the course. If I ask you: "Should the court dismiss for reason X?" your answer must focus on *reason X*. Do not discuss anything else. The question was specific, and your answer must be specific too. Exam answers that do not answer the question asked will not be passing exam answers. Discussing topics that are not relevant to the question asked is wasting time. You will not earn points for those discussions.

F. Read the Facts (and Again)

After you have read the call of the question, read the fact pattern. You should read it once. Then you should read it again. And perhaps again. Understanding the facts may be the most important part of the exam. In a one-hour exam question, the first five to ten minutes should be spent just reading the exam and ensuring that you understand what is being asked. Consider highlighting, circling, or underlining key points or facts in the exam. If a fact is included in the question you should likely discuss or use it in your answer. A common mistake by law students is to not talk enough about the facts in their exam answers. Law professors want students to talk about the law in a particular factual context. So spending time to carefully read and understand the question's fact pattern is time well spent.

G. Outline Your Answer

You have read the instructions, allocated your time, read the call of the question and the facts carefully—now you should outline your answer. You must spend time thinking through your answer before you start writing. Doing so will help you spot the key issues and organize your answer. Students who organize their answer, almost always do better on exams. A short outline ensures that: (1) you don't forget to discuss key points you intend to discuss; and (2) you stay organized.

You will feel pressure to start writing immediately. Don't. Even if the person next to you starts madly tapping away at the keyboard, you will ensure that you've spent a few minutes thinking through your answer and how to organize it. As a rule of thumb, in a one-hour essay exam, your total time for reading the call, reading the facts, and outlining should take approximately 15 minutes. You must leave enough time (at least 45 minutes) to write your answer.

Students who do not outline spend pages discussing the issues in a meandering way, often describing obscure and unlikely arguments. Students who have spent time outlining know that four or five issues must be covered and the time they have to cover each issue. Those students are far more likely to provide an analysis that adheres to the relevant legal and factual issues and will do well. An exam answer that is a stream of consciousness will not do well. Exams are not about getting down as much on paper as possible. Professors do not like to read a roller-coaster of an answer. I especially don't like them, and have been known to lash out viciously when I read an exam written this way. You must provide an organized and logical response to the question asked.

Of course, some students overcompensate. An exam outline is short, it should not be a lengthy or intricate summary of your answer. Do not write out every rule or every fact that you will later discuss. Do not write out every legal topics mentioned in the course either. Instead jot down the main issues that the essay question raises in the order you will address them. Generally, an outlined answer will revolve around the elements of the claim—the different points of law you must analyze to answer the question asked.

Writing the Exam

How should you write a law school exam? Professors have differing advice. But here are a few tips that most commonly agree on.

A. Use Headings

Professors hate grading. Grading cuts into time that we could be writing, researching, speaking at conferences, preparing for class, spending time with family, or taking a vacation. Professors don't have time, and won't make time, to suss out every point that you made or could have made on your exam. In short, you must make it simple for your professor to follow your analysis. This means you must use headings and subheadings to break up the different issues in the exam. Headings make your exam answer easier to read and will reveal your logical organization.

As a general rule, you should have one main heading for each issue that the call of the question asks you to analyze. You should also use subheadings for each element of the rule that addresses the issue. Any exam in my course that does not use headings and subheadings will receive a poor grade. I do not care how sophisticated your legal analysis is. In my experience, if you don't use headings, you will do poorly.

B. Use IRAC

When writing an exam, use "IRAC." IRAC is acronym that stands for Issue, Rule, Analysis, and Conclusion. IRAC is a useful tool for organizing an answer to a law school essay exam, and a method of legal analysis. Some law professors prefer variations on IRAC, such as "CRAC—Conclusion, Rule, Analysis, Conclusion" or "IRRAC—Issue, Rule, Rule Explanation, Analysis, Conclusion."

The basic IRAC structure is fairly straightforward: for each legal issue raised, you must set out the legal principles and rules before you apply those legal rules to the facts of the question. Said differently, for each question asked in an exam, spot and identify the relevant legal issues, explain what law relates to those issues, and then analyze the facts in light of the law to draw a reasoned conclusion. You must explain why the facts show that certain elements or rules have been met or not met.

C. Write Precise and Succinct Rules

When writing an exam, you must have the applicable law down cold. You must set out the law (the rules, test, factors etc.) clearly, succinctly, and precisely. Some study guides recommend you skip the rules and incorporate them in your answer. Don't listen to them. Unless your professor tells you otherwise, this is terrible advice. You must for each issue and sub-issue carefully set out the rules that you intend to apply.

Precision in law matters. It is not okay to get the rule "kind of right." "Kind of right" is equal to wrong. Half-right rule summaries do not earn points. Professors generally do not require specific case names, but if you're referring to a case, say enough about the facts to identify the case. If you're applying a test, rule, formula, or the like, you should set it forth clearly and accurately in the exam.

D. Use the Facts, All of Them

Facts are critical. Legal analysis boils down to discussing the law in the context of particular facts. Lawyers get paid to identify relevant facts from irrelevant facts, and then apply the law to the facts. For this reason, an answer that merely recites canned rules or cases is deficient. Exams that also just state conclusions will earn a low grade too. Rather, to earn a top grade you must apply the rules to the facts. You must demonstrate you understand the nuances of the facts and the relevance of the details. You must explain why you reach the conclusions you did.

Do not simply restate or summarize the facts. I wrote the exam. I know what I wrote. Show me that you understand why certain facts are significant and why the facts of the particular problem lead you to a particular conclusion. In short, argue from the facts. Professors spend considerable time incorporating key facts in an exam question. You must be certain to incorporate them and discuss them in your answer.

E. Use the Word *Because*

You must explain how you reach your conclusions. A conclusion without a reason is worth very few points. Professors are much more concerned with how you justify the conclusions you reach. Use the word *because* liberally. Doing so ensures that you demonstrate that you understand the legal concepts and how to apply them in the particular circumstances asked for in the exam.

F. Argue Both Sides

For most law school exams you will have to analyze a number of legal issues. For many (but not all) of these issues, the professor will have made the question a "close call." In these circumstances you must provide the differing arguments that could be made, and then explain why you think one side of the argument will prevail over the other. Too many students lose objectivity and argue for only one side. You won't. You will argue both sides.

Don't misunderstand. Arguing both sides does not mean that you can avoid answering the question asked. You must provide a conclusion, and tell the professor which arguments are strong and which are weak. Too often students write a on-the-one-hand on-the-other-hand examination, without reaching a conclusion. Good lawyers exercise judgment, and good exam answers should demonstrate that the student can exercise judgment too. While many exams may have more than one reasonable "right answer," professors want you to draw a conclusion and justify why you reached that conclusion.

G. Emphasize Policy

Law school exams are not primarily designed to test policy, or other esoteric arguments about law that you may have discussed in class. The bread and butter of most law school exams is to apply legal knowledge to a new set of facts. That said, the very best answers to law school exams incorporate policy considerations into the answer.

Demonstrate to your professor that you understand the nuance behind the law and that on close questions you recognize that the so-called black-letter never provides a clear answer. To do this, explain how policy considerations inform why you reach the conclusion you do.

H. Use Plain English

This is not the time for Shakespearean prose. But you must write clearly. A sloppy exam with fragments or run-on sentences, and many typographical and grammatical mistakes is difficult to read. Most professors will not grade on writing style. But the best-written, most organized exams are often also the strongest substantive exams. Use plain English, and write short, easy-to-follow, declarative sentences.

You will not write a law school exam as if you are "IM'ing" your BFF. You will not use abbreviations. Yes, an exam is time pressured. But you will write your answer in complete English. "U" is not acceptable for "you." Never write a sentence like: "The I is whether the CT has PJ over D, when P brought the claim in CA." I don't read alphabet soup. If you "IM" me, I will IM you back with a simple "F." Although you are using "IRAC," do not label the different parts of your analysis with I, R, A, and C.

I. Write Enough

A common blunder for new students is to underestimate how much a student must write to do well on a law school essay exam. The longest answers certainly aren't the best, but very short answers rarely are able to sufficiently address the issues raised in the exam. A student who turns in one or two double-spaced pages in response to an hour long essay exam is almost certainly guaranteeing themselves a poor (perhaps failing) grade.

Although very short answers will not do well, precision and economy matters. Long-rambling answers invariably do poorly. The student who madly "vomits on the page" all information they know about the course is guaranteed a mediocre grade. Strong exam answers are lean and focused, with every word included for a reason.

J. Avoid Humor

As a general rule, using humor in your exam answer is almost always a mistake. The professor takes the exam questions seriously and grades the exams seriously—you should take it seriously too. Humor is rarely appropriate. This is not the time to be funny or sarcastic. Trust me. Humor in an exam does not earn you any additional points. At best, all it does is waste valuable time. At worst, it could hurt you and oftentimes seems strained.

K. Use Common Sense

Don't forget common sense. You don't want to become an automaton, flooding your exam answers with canned nonsense that leads to ridiculous results. Keep your common sense and gut instincts. If you conclude that the court should strike as unconstitutional some long-standing (and previously unchallenged) law, or that a court should punish some innocuous activity with years imprisonment, or your conclusion would lead to societal chaos and cause mass disruption, you should pause (at least for a moment). The very best law students don't toss their judgment at the exam door.

Learning by Example

Let me give you an example to illustrate the difference between a weak and a strong exam answer. Assume you have an exam question where a plaintiff is suing for negligence. The negligence claim arose after the defendant allegedly drove into plaintiff's car on a busy street: defendant was speeding and talking on his cell phone. The accident injured both the plaintiff and the defendant, and they were taken to a local hospital. Several hours later, the plaintiff saw the defendant in the hospital and, in front of several doctors, punched him in the nose screaming, "I can't believe you ruined my new car."

Assume one of the legal issues in the exam is whether the civil assault claim (defendant's claim against plaintiff for punching him) is a compulsory counterclaim. Compulsory counterclaims are claims that arise from the "same transaction or occurrence" as the underlying claim. In determining whether claims arise from the "same transaction or occurrence," courts usually ask whether there exists a logical relationship between the two claims where separate trials on each of the claims would involve a substantial duplication of effort and time by the parties and the courts.

Here are four sample answers to this issue.

Exam Answer #1

The assault claim is a probably a compulsory counter-claim. I think the two claims are logically connected to one another Defendant may disagree and say, *inter alia*, that the claims are not logically connected, and a judge might agree with the defendant. But it's unlikely. Clearly in the case at bar this is compulsory counterclaim.

Put me out of my misery: kill me now. This answer is worth almost no points. It says nothing. Absolutely nothing. It doesn't directly tell you what the legal issue is, nor does it set forth a rule summary, and it doesn't apply the rules to the facts. The legal rule that the student uses is incorrect ("logically connected" instead of "logically related"). Worse yet, the student uses legalese in an attempt to sound lawyerly, without saying anything ("inter alia," "the case at bar"). Nowhere does the student provide a reason for the conclusion. The use of the word "clearly" is also a mistake. A clear answer does not exist. The fact the student thinks there is one betrays the student's misunderstanding of the law.

Exam Answer #2

The issue is whether the assault claim is a compulsory counterclaim because it arose from the same transaction or occurrence as the plaintiff's negligence claim. Compulsory counterclaims are governed under Rule 13 of the Federal Rules of Civil Procedure. In class, we talked about the history behind and purpose behind compulsory counterclaims. Requiring that compulsory counterclaims be brought in one suit makes a great deal of sense because courts are congested, and it's very costly to have separate trials on a whole bunch of issues. And if you're a judge, you'd want to hear the same case only once. This is the point Justice Brennan made in the case we read.

Compulsory counterclaims are also what the *Smith* case talks about in detail. In that case, the court found that compulsory counterclaims are claims that arise from the same transaction or occurrence. The court found that a defamation claim did not arise out of the same events as a negligence claim. There was a dissent that disagreed, but the majority found the defamation claim was not a compulsory counterclaim. [Professor, you said the same thing in class—compulsory counterclaims arise from the same transaction or occurrence].

This is also a close call. (I knew you would write a tough exam question Prof. Lawrence, I just knew it! But I've got this one figured out ☺—thanks for a good class by the

way.) And reasonable minds can differ. But I think the
court would likely find they arose from the same event
(i.e, the car accident). It certainly would be better to have
one trial than two here. It's exactly what the *Smith* case
said.

Aaagh. This is worse. Although this student sets out a rule summary (sort-of), they don't apply the rules to the facts of this case.
No analysis exists at all. The writer only draws a conclusion—this
is not legal analysis.

Don't let the long answer fool you. This tells you even less than
the prior answer. The example is the "tell-you-everything-I-know-
about-the-class" approach that served students well in college, but
will earn you very low grades in law school. The student talks a lot
about counterclaims in general, but does not spend much time explaining why there is or is not a compulsory counterclaim in this
particular case. The student does not answer the question asked.
Finally, the attempt to curry favor at the end will anger many professors.

Exam Answer #3

The issue is whether the assault claim is a compulsory
counterclaim. Compulsory counterclaims are claims that
arise from the same transaction or occurrence. In determining whether claims arise from the "same transaction
or occurrence," courts ask if a logical relationship exists
between the two claims where separate trials on each of
the claims would involve a substantial duplication of effort and time by the parties and the courts. In this case,
the claims seem to be related because they both have to
do with the car accident. Plaintiff punched defendant because of the accident. Therefore, the court will likely find
the assault claim to be compulsory.

Okay, not bad. This is better and is perhaps an average or perhaps slightly below average answer. The student starts off by identifying the legal issue and setting out an accurate rule summary.

The student falls short though in the factual analysis. The student discusses only two facts (that the claims have to do with the car accident, and that "plaintiff punched defendant because of the accident"). The student does not acknowledge any nuance in the answer, and does not note plausible counter-arguments.

Exam Answer #4

1. Is the Assault Claim a Compulsory Counterclaim?

The issue is whether the assault claim is a compulsory counterclaim. Compulsory counterclaims are claims against opposing parties that arise from the same transaction or occurrence. In determining this, courts ask if a logical relationship exists between the two claims where separate trials on each of the claims would involve a substantial duplication of effort and time by the parties and the courts.

Here, the two claims likely arose from the same transaction or occurrence. The two events occurred about the same time (the accident occurred only a few hours earlier than the punching) and involved the same event (the car accident). But for the car accident, the plaintiff and defendant would not have been in the hospital and the plaintiff would not have punched defendant in the nose. The facts say the reason the plaintiff punched the defendant was because the defendant "ruined his car." The parties to both claims are the same. *Because* of all these facts, there seems to be a logical connection between the two events so that it would make sense for a jury to hear the two claims together.

On the other hand, this may not be a compulsory counterclaim *because* it's unclear that a separate trial on the assault claim would involve a substantial duplication of effort and time. The punching occurred at a different place than the accident (hospital, not busy street), at a different time (several hours later), and involved different witnesses (the doctors, instead of witnesses on the busy street). The evidence in the negligence case would involve whether the defendant was speeding or talking on his cell phone, while the assault claim would focus on what the plaintiff did in the hospital. Because the evidence and witnesses will be different, substantial duplication should not occur if the claims were heard separately.

Which argument will persuade the court is uncertain. Given, however, the increasing congestion in courts and the perception that too many lawsuits are filed, a judge may be more likely to find that the two claims must be brought together and that the assault claim is compulsory.

Finally, here's a strong answer. I would give it an A. After a clear heading, it starts off by identifying the issue, followed by a precise and correct rule summary. The rule summary identifies the rules (same transaction or occurrence, logical relationship) and the reason for the rule (avoids duplication). The analysis points to specific facts to explain why the student concludes that claims are logically related and then provides a counter-argument. Notice how the student argues both sides and used the word *because*. The student then ends with a conclusion that touches on a policy implication—the congestion in the courts.

Emergencies and After the Exam

If you have studied, kept up with class throughout the semester and taken practice exams, you'll do fine. What happens though in situations when things don't go fine....

A. If Your Mind Blanks

Often essay exams will have more than one essay questions (or at least several calls of the question). What should you do if your mind simply goes blank and you don't understand what is being asked, or if you have no idea how to answer the question?

In these situations, the most important thing is not to panic. Take a deep breath. And then take another. After you've done that, look at the call of the question again, and in your mind go through a checklist of the main topics covered in the course. Do any of them apply? Often going through the outline of topics in your mind will cause you hit upon what the professor is asking.

If after a few minutes, you still have no idea—move on. Go onto the next essay question. Don't waste more time. You can always go back. Moving on will reduce your anxiety and it may well be that the second question is easier to answer. After answering another question, when you return you may well see the question in a new light.

B. If All Else Fails

Sometimes, however, no matter how well prepared you are, you might have a "freak-out" moment and can't spot any issues on the exam. This rarely happens for students who have prepared properly. Students who are prepared usually will understand what the professor is looking for. But what happens if you can't understand the first question, and after flipping to the second you don't understand it either? The entire exam is now reading like a foreign language. And even after taking some deep breaths and some time to reflect, you have no idea what to do. You've been whipped into a frenzy and are tempted to run from the exam room screaming pulling out your hair as you go. You suspect, however, that doing so may guarantee you a failing grade not to mention a special place in the school's urban legends for years to come.

If all else fails start going through the main topics or legal issues covered in the course and write short IRACs, applying the facts of the question, to each topic. There's two reasons for doing this. First, after writing out several topics, you may hit upon an issue that actually is relevant to the question or otherwise spur you to spot analysis the professor is looking for. Sometimes just writing will calm you down and allow you to focus and pass the "freak-out" moment. Second, at least you're giving the professor something. If you turn in an exam with no writing, the professor has no choice but to give you a failing grade. If you write out the main topics covered in the class the professor may take mercy and give you some sympathy-points that will pull you above the passing line.

C. A Few Nevers

Two absolute "nevers" after law school exams. First, never talk about the substantive aspects of the exam with your friends after the exam is over. It's done. Move on. It's time to focus on the next exam. Talking about the exam will only increase your anxiety as you discover issues that you may have missed. What's worse is you may not have missed the issue at all—it may be that your friend misread the question. But you'll never know. By talking with friends, you guarantee stressing yourself out. Keep the discussion generic (e.g., "that was a tough exam!").

Second, whatever you do, do not call your professor to discuss how you did on the exam before the professors submits the course grades. Calling your professor is unprofessional. Usually professors grade anonymously. Providing a professor with any information about how you answered the exam question destroys that anonymity.

Another point. How well you performed on an exam is nearly impossible to predict. For most schools, law school grades are curved. You receive a grade not on how well you did in absolute terms, but on how well you did relative to your classmates. Your grade, therefore, will not necessarily correlate to how well you thought you performed. If an exam felt particularly difficult, don't be surprised if you scored very well. It may mean that you were just less lost on the exam than your classmates. Similarly, you may not do as well on an exam that you thought was quite easy—it may have been easy for all your classmates too.

D. Self-Assessment

At some point you will receive your grade and your exam at many schools will be available for collecting. Many students never collect their exams—you will. After each exam, retrieve the exam and assess what you did well and what you didn't do well. If the professor has provided a cut sheet or an answer key, this should be fairly easy to do. If the professor has not provided a cut sheet or answer key, then consider making an appointment to see the professor. This is not the time to grade-grub (i.e., never argue that you should have received a higher grade), but asking the professor for insight into how you could have done better is appropriate.

E. Final Words on Exams and Grades

A common question students ask is how important are law school grades? In the short term, first-year grades can be very important. The stakes are high. Employers need an easy way to assess potential applicants, and grades are considered an easy proxy for your potential as a lawyer. If your goal is to work in a very large, so-called elite law firm, grades for most law schools are critical to getting your foot in the door. A slate of straight As is also probably necessary to have any chance to clerk for a federal appellate court or the U.S. Supreme Court. And there's your pride too. There's something unsettling when you find out you didn't do as well as the irritating schlub in the front row who flubbed every question asked when called on in class.

But law school grades are probably also much less important than many think. First, your law school GPA is often completely irrelevant after your first job. Once you have graduated, employers are much more concerned with whether you are a good attorney than what your law school GPA was. Second, for most law students at most law schools, jobs are obtained through networking and alumni connections. In those circumstances, while strong grades are helpful, other criteria often comes into play. Third, grades may be key to obtaining a screening interview, but after that your ability to interview in a professional way and your personality is substantially more important. Plenty of stories exist of the very top student with the highest grades struggling to obtain a job because of social awkwardness or an inability to interview well.

That's it. That's all the advice I have. Follow it and you'll do fine."

* * * * *

Yikes! I was feeling a little numb and even a little depressed. What had I gotten myself into. Here were my notes. I was going to review these again carefully:

Preparing for Final Exams

☐ Know the exam details (is it open, closed, how many questions, how long...)
☐ Read the school's exam rules (what can you bring into the exam)
☐ Review prior exams given by professor
☐ Keep outlines updated on a weekly basis
☐ Schedule practice exams early and often (don't wait until the end of the semester!)
☐ Take some practice exams under timed conditions
☐ Learn how professor grades for each course
☐ Go to any review sessions
☐ Take advantage of Academic Support
☐ Learn the law (rule summaries) by heart

The Day of the Exam

☐ Arrive early
☐ Arrive prepared (pens, pencils, highlighters, pencil sharpeners, erasers, analog clock, snacks, if permitted)
☐ Don't cram
☐ Dress in layers and comfortably
☐ Test laptop before exam to ensure it's working properly

Starting the Exam

☐ Read the exam instructions carefully
☐ Allocate time among questions
☐ Read the call of the question
☐ Read the facts carefully (a few times)
☐ Outline the answer

Writing the Exam

☐ Stay calm and breathe
☐ No preambles—answer the question asked. Get right to it!
☐ Use headings
☐ Use IRAC (rules before analysis)
☐ Write precise, succinct rules
☐ Use the facts (all of them)
☐ Explain conclusions and significance of facts (use the word "because")
☐ Argue both sides
☐ Emphasize policy considerations
☐ Write clearly and legibly
☐ Don't use humor (be professional)
☐ Use common sense (watch out for crazy conclusions!)

After the Exam

☐ Don't talk about the exam's substance right after the exam (no exam debrief with friends)
☐ Don't pester the professor
☐ Pick up exams after they are graded
☐ Do a self-assessment after you receive your grade (how could you have improved)
☐ Visit professor for guidance, but no grade-grubbing!
☐ Keep it all in perspective

Chapter 7

Outside of Class

It was the Spring semester and we were sitting in Professor's Lawrence's class, a few weeks away from finals. Soon we would be finished the first year. We were feeling the pressure: keeping up with class reading, preparing outlines, taking practice exams, and reviewing notes were eating up our days. None of us had a moment to spare. It was intense. Black circles under the eyes had become a fashion statement and our own badge of courage. At this point in the semester we were swimming as fast as we could to just to keep our heads above water. Surprise—Professor Lawrence took this priceless moment to give us more to do!

"Wake up kids. I see you're tired, you're stressed, and some of you look overwhelmed. So what? You knew it wouldn't be easy. But let me tell you now: after you finish your first year, you've got more to do.

Although most of you are spending every waking minute with your nose buried in your case book—studying can not define your law school experience. If case briefs and outlines represent the totality of your law school years, you will look back on them with regret. Law school is more than just studying. You need to participate in extracurricular or co-curricular activities. Both are essential to developing professional skills and building a resume that will land you a legal job. These are the activities that will allow you to explore your interests, develop your legal skills, cultivate important connections in the legal community, and make some genuine friends. When you look back on your law school days, the activities outside class are the ones that you will be the most proud of and you will reminisce about. More importantly, employers these days don't hire students who only spend time in class. You have to get involved and build your resume.

Each school is different. The most common extra- and co-curricular activities, however, include joining a law journal, competing in advocacy honors programs, participating in an externship or a legal clinic, working for professors, and devoting time to public and community service. Students also commonly become involved with a variety of student organizations and clubs. Most students will participate in several of these activities while in law school.

Law Journals (and Law Review)

The infamous Law Review. Is it all that it is made out to be? Maybe. If you want to become a law professor or a judicial clerk for a prestigious federal judge, then most likely yes. Even if your interests lie in private practice, public interest, or with government, law review is likely to open doors. And the experience one gets from being a Law Review or a law journal member can be a valuable experience. Being on Law Review doesn't mean that you're destined to be god's gift to the legal profession, but it can be useful to have on your resume.

Here's an overview of what law journals are, how you become a member, and why being a law journal member can be a valuable experience.

A. What Are They?

Law journals are academic journals that publish academic articles written mostly by professors, but also by private practitioners, judges, government officials, and other legal professionals. These articles commonly attempt to explain trends in the law, explore a particularly troublesome area of the law, or describe the theoretical underpinnings of particular legal rules or court decisions. Law journals also often host symposia to explore a particular hot issue in the law, and will publish student articles, usually called "notes" or "comments."

Unlike legal journal in other countries, in the United States the vast majority of law journals are student run and edited. Most law journals will have an Executive Board of third-year students (or upper-division part-time students) that are responsible for the day-to-day administration. Second-year students edit the articles, and ensure that the article's footnote sources are properly cited in both form and substance (a process known as cite-checking).

Different kinds of law journals exist. A school's main publication often (but not always) has "Law Review" in its title, and is commonly referred to just as the Law Review (e.g., the *Harvard Law Review*, the *Yale Law Journal*). The Law Review publishes articles on a wide variety of topics and is considered the school's flagship publication. Increasingly, however, schools also have a number of other specialty journals. These journals usually focus on a particular area of law, such as animal law, business or corporate law, children's rights, entertainment, environment, human rights, labor, gender and race issues, or international law (e.g., the *Stanford Journal of International Law*, the *Columbia Journal of Gender and Law*). A small number of journals focus on regulatory, statutory, or public policy issues (e.g., the *NYU Journal of Legislation & Public Policy*). At schools with multiple law reviews, membership on the main law review is commonly considered the most prestigious.

B. How Do You Become a Member?

The criteria for becoming a member of Law Review or a specialty law journal vary from school to school. Usually students become members in their second year. Some law reviews will extend membership invitations based solely on first-year grades. Most school's law reviews, however, will select members based on a combination of a student's first-year grades and performance in a "write-on competition." The write-on competition often requires students to write a small paper in a discrete period of time. Some law reviews also require that students complete an editing exercise. Sometimes the write-on competition occurs during the spring semester, although more commonly the competition occurs either immediately after spring final exams or in the summer.

While standards vary, success in the write-on competition requires rigorous legal analysis, clear writing, and meticulous footnoting. Students who wish to secure a place on their school's law review should consider reading a book on academic writing and law review competitions before the competition begins. Students should also know the citation rules that the law review follows (usually the bluebook). Two good guides that provide a detailed overview are: Eugene Volokh, *Academic Legal Writing: Law Review Articles, Student Notes, Seminar Papers, and Getting on Law Review* (3d ed. 2007) and Elizabeth Fajans & Mary R. Falk, *Scholarly Writing for Law Students: Seminar Papers, Law Review Notes and Law Review Competition Papers* (3d ed. 2004).

C. Should You Try?

Being a member of a law journal is a lot of work. Yet it has its benefits. First, it's a good experience. Students on Law Review spend hours doing the kind of in-depth, meticulous legal research and writing that is required of attorneys and law clerks. Law review will help you hone your ability to write effectively and to use the blue book citation manual. Law Review members are also trained to pay close attention to detail. These are skills that you'll use as an attorney.

Second, Law Review membership is a credential that makes your resume look pretty. And it will stay that way. If you're a Law Review member, your resume will always say "Law Review" (not so, for other activities in law school, which may disappear from your resume once you get more practical experience). For many employers, law journal membership is seen as a proxy for good grades and strong writing skills. At the very least, employers know that law journal is a rigorous experience. Law Review memberships means you have likely had more practice editing, proofreading, cite-checking, and writing than other students.

On the other hand, keeping the experience in perspective is important. Working as a law journal member is time consuming and can be stressful. Most who join consider quitting at least a few times before the semester is done. Students who have families or who are working and attending law school part-time, will find participating in law journals particularly challenging. Although law journal membership is valuable to have on your resume, other things in life are simply more important. Remaining married, seeing your kids grow up, and being able to afford a roof over your head certainly trump any value law journal can bring to your life.

D. Once You Are Accepted

A law journal's membership is most commonly divided into staff members and editors. On most law journals, second-year students are the staff, while third-year students serve as senior editors, including the editor-in-chief, executive editor, managing editor, senior articles editor, and senior notes or comments editor.

Your year as a law journal staff member normally will consist of three different types of work. First, as a member you will be responsible for editing, proofreading, and cite-checking articles that the law review is publishing. Usually you will do this under the supervision of a third-year student. Your main responsibility will be to ensure that the references authors rely on support the author's claims and are in proper Bluebook (or possibly ALWD) format.

Second, the journal will likely require that you write a student Note or Comment. Notes and Comments are student-written pieces of legal scholarship that are typically shorter than the articles that faculty write and submit. A Note is intended to discuss and analyze a discrete, focused legal issue or problem in depth. A Comment analyzes a recent case or piece of legislation. Some law journals will also permit students to write book reviews. Usually Notes and Comments will be under 15,000 word long, and sometimes shorter (faculty written articles vary in length but are commonly between 25,000–35,000 words). Write to impress. If you produce a well-written, interesting, original, and adequately supported Note or Comment you may receive an invitation to publish the Note or Comment in one of the school's law journals.

Lastly, you may assist in hosting a symposium or conference. This can include planning the symposium, inviting speakers, and then working with speakers as they submit symposium articles.

Working on a symposium can be a tremendous amount of work, but often will give you the opportunity to interact with faculty from other schools, judges, or practitioners with expertise in a particular area of law.

E. Board Positions and the Third Year

At the end of your second year, you may have the opportunity to apply for an executive board position. Third year law students run the administration of the law review. Executive board positions commonly consist of the Editor-in-Chief, an Executive or Managing Editor, a Lead Articles Editor, a Lead Notes and Comments Editor, and other positions. Each journal has its own rules and customs, but usually articles editors select and edit articles, notes and comments editors work with students on their written work, and managing and executive editors supervise staff in the cite-checking, proofreading, and formatting of articles.

Working on a board in your third year will keep you busy. You're responsible for ensuring that the journal runs smoothly. But a board position is a nice credential that looks good on a resume and can be a good learning experience.

F. Maintain Perspective

One last note: failure to make the Law Review or law journal is not the end of your law career. Law Review is a good experience, but you can become a very successful lawyer without ever participating in Law Review. Build your resume in other ways. Participate in moot court. Participate in trial advocacy programs. Become a research assistant for your professor. All of these activities are attractive to employers as well, and some—even if considered less prestigious—may provide you better training for being a lawyer.

Advocacy Programs

Practical skills programs, such as moot court and trial advocacy, offer hands-on experience. If you are not participating in a law journal (and even if you are) you should consider joining one of these programs.

A. What Are They?

Most schools will offer students the opportunity to participate in extra-curricular advocacy programs. The three most common are: (1) moot court (appellate advocacy); (2) mock trial (trial advocacy); and (3) negotiation or arbitration.

In moot court, students prepare and argue a case before an appellate court. Although programs differ, commonly students will write an appellate brief and then participate in a simulated appellate oral argument. Oral argument is presented to a panel of three judges, with arguments ranging from ten to thirty minutes a person. The judges are commonly law professors, and members of the bench and bar. Students in a moot court honors program will likely compete as an oralist or a brief writer in regional, national, and sometimes international interscholastic competitions.

In mock trial (trial advocacy) programs, students participate in simulated trial court proceedings and focus on developing particular litigation skills. These programs can be either civil or criminal-law focused and require students to prepare a case for trial, to create a case strategy, and to use the rules of evidence in a simulated trial experience. Mock trial programs will teach you how to make an opening statement and a closing argument, conduct a direct and cross examination, and assert evidentiary objections. In a mock trial program, volunteers usually serve as witnesses, jurors, and the judge. As with moot court, trial advocacy programs often compete in regional and national competitions.

In negotiation programs, students are given practical opportunities to hone their negotiation, dispute management, and conflict resolution skills. Negotiation programs, although less common than moot court and mock trial programs, are increasingly being embraced by law schools because of the practical training they provide. As with moot court and trial advocacy programs, students will often compete in simulated negotiation exercises that are held in regional and national competitions.

For some schools, students must enroll in a course as a condition for being a member of an advocacy program. For moot court, students may be required to take an advanced writing or oral advocacy course. For trial advocacy programs, students often participate in advanced evidence and trial practice courses that have simulation components to them. For negotiation programs, students may be asked to enroll in specialized interviewing, counseling, and negotiation courses.

B. How Do You Become a Member?

Usually schools consider advocacy programs as honor programs with strict selection criteria. Each program will have its own selection criteria and criteria differs among schools. Most commonly, however, students are selected based on performance in an intramural competition and a student's first-year grades. Usually students must be in good academic standing to participate. Often these advocacy programs are student run with some limited faculty or alumni oversight.

As with law journals, students usually apply for a position in an advocacy program at the end of their first year of law school or over the first-year summer. Students are then members during their second year, with the opportunity to become a senior advocacy or a member of an Executive Board during their third year.

C. Should You Try?

You should give serious thought to participating in an advocacy program. One of the main goals of any law school experience should be to develop lawyering skills that will help you enter the profession. Advocacy programs are uniquely well-suited opportunities for developing some "real-world" skills. Participation in an advocacy program will also often allow you to develop closer relationships with faculty (both adjunct and full-time) and with alumni. It's not uncommon to hear of students being offered jobs after impressing a mock judge in a competition.

Which program is right for you? Think about your goals after law school. If your career plan involves appellate practice or working in a large law firm, then moot court may be a good choice. Moot court usually provides a significant writing experience, which is useful for most areas of practice. If you plan on being a prosecutor, a city attorney, or a public defender, then you may wish to consider trial advocacy. Trial advocacy programs provide the best training for students who plan to focus on trial work and expect to be in court a lot after graduation. If you plan on developing a transactional practice, then a negotiation program may be a good choice to help you develop a skills base to go into a business or real estate practice. No right answer exists, and all three programs develop important skills for almost any practice area.

Regardless of the program you choose, all will provide you with practical experience. You will receive valuable feedback from practicing attorneys as well as be given opportunities for networking. Employers look for participation in skills programs and, when they don't see it, they are likely to ask you why you did not participate. Having said all that, the real reason to join these programs is because they are tremendous fun. So join something! Make the most of your time in law school. You will come out of school with skills and confidence that will serve you well in the job market and in your practice. You do not later want to be asking yourself, or worse, have an employer ask you, "What the heck did you do with your time?"

Externships and Clinics

Upper-division students should actively seek out opportunities for practical training to learn the skills, habits, and techniques that are necessary to succeed in the legal profession. Students also want to make connections with the local legal community. Two other good ways of doing so is through externships or working in a legal clinic.

A. An Introduction to Externships

Many schools have externship programs that allow students to gain legal experience for credit, rather than pay. Externships occur outside the law school and in a format that usually does not involve attendance at regularly scheduled class sessions. Externship programs assist law schools in meeting their overall educational objectives by permitting students to practically apply the legal knowledge gained in the classroom.

The types of externships and their structure can vary. Externship placements may be with judges, in-house legal departments, public interest organizations, or federal, state and local government offices. Only in exceptional circumstances are externships offered with private law firms and other for-profit organizations. Externships usually are a semester long or in the summer and, in many schools, students can enroll in both part-time and full-time externships. Occasionally, students can enroll in a full-time externship abroad. Demand for, and participation in, externships have increased significantly in recent years in schools across the country.

Students should seek out externship opportunities for a number of reasons. First, externships provide students with a unique opportunity to be immersed in hands-on, practical legal training and experiential learning. Second, externships provide students an opportunity to build connections in the legal community and gain a better understanding of real-life law practice. Externships allow students to make connections that could lead to full-time employment. For highly-competitive public interest jobs, an externship may almost be a prerequisite for a job after graduation. Increasingly, an externship is considered a good leg up to getting any job in a tough legal market. Externships can be a great resume builder. Not surprisingly, a legal externship is much more impressive on your resume than Starbucks or a trip to Europe.

B. An Introduction to Clinics

Legal clinics are law school programs that provide hands-on-legal experience to students under close supervision. The clinic usually occupies a physical space that is either in the law school or near to it. A full-time clinical faculty member will usually direct and be responsible for overseeing and supervising the student members, and is often supported by some administrative staff (paralegals, social workers, secretaries, etc.). Clinics typically do public service and community-based work, providing free legal services to the indigent and underserved populations. The area of specialization for clinics vary dramatically. Some common clinic focuses include animal law, bankruptcy, children's rights, community law, criminal defense, domestic violence, elder law, employment and wage claims, environmental, family, human rights, immigration, landlord/tenant, mediation, small business, street law, and tax.

The work a student can expect in a clinical experience also varies depending on the clinic's focus. Students will typically provide assistance with legal research, writing memorandum, and drafting legal documents, as well as client-intake, and meeting and interviewing clients or witnesses. In many jurisdictions, courts have "student practice" rules that allow clinic students to be certified and then appear and argue in court or before an administrative law judge. Often a classroom component (such as a clinic seminar or clinic course) will provide students with the necessary foundation and background in the relevant law.

Clinical experiences are usually offered during the fall or spring semester of the second and third year. Students should make it a priority to enroll in a clinic prior to graduation as not only a way to do community service, but as a way to develop practical lawyering skills that will be useful upon graduation. Legal clinical experience is valued by employers and looks great on a resume. Clinics are known to be selective in the students they choose, and allow chosen students to develop relationships with mentors in an intimate environment. That intimate environment with top-notch attorneys has the potential to open doors for students.

Other Opportunities

After the first year, students have more time to dedicate to activities outside the classroom. Students should look into opportunities that interest them, without spreading themselves too thin. Here is an overview of what some of those opportunities are:

A. Teaching and Research Assistant Positions

Yes, the opportunity you have all been waiting for with bated breath … the chance to work for me (and for the less fortunate, other professors). Most professors will hire upper-division students either to assist with a course (i.e., as a teaching assistant) or with research on an article or book project that the professor is working on (i.e., as a research assistant).

This is something you should not pass up. After all, I am the expert in my field and will likely provide you with a golden opportunity to work on a new and upcoming legal issue. This is my way of assisting you in your job search. Imagine this: you work for me researching the newest intellectual property issue; you then go and interview with an intellectual property firm and are able to discuss this up to date issue with the practicing attorneys—maybe even know something they don't! All because of my expertise.

And the excitement doesn't end there. You will also develop a professional relationship with me. You continuously complain that it is too easy to get lost in the shuffle of law school; that there is no personal attention. Well, working for me gives you a once in a life time opportunity to get that attention you have been longing for. You will have a personal guide as to how you are advancing in your ability to perform research and legal analysis. And perhaps most importantly—unlike externships, clinics, law journals or advocacy programs—you will get paid. Most professors are able to pay students to serve as teaching and research assistants through federal work study or other faculty funds.

B. Student Organizations

Most law schools have literally dozens and dozens of student organizations and groups that students can participate in. These organizations are based on social, political, service and professional interests and will hold almost daily events. Student organizations provide a good way for students to meet and get to know other students with similar backgrounds, interests, or goals.

Schools will often have 20–40 different student organizations and their focus will be varied. Some groups focus on substantive areas of the law (e.g., the Business Law Association, the Criminal Law Society, the Environmental Law Society, International Law Society, Intellectual Property Law Society, etc.), while others are politically or religiously focused (e.g., the Federalist Society, the Christian Legal Society, the Muslim Law Students Association, the Democratic or Republican Student Associations, etc.), and others are based on social or ethnic groups (e.g., the Black Law Students Association, the Native American Law Students Association, the Older Wiser Law Students Association, OUTlaws, the Latino Law Students Association, the Women's Law Association, etc.). Some are purely social in nature or sponsor intramural sports (e.g., the Golf Association or the Law and Wine Society). Some schools will have a student-run newspaper or a Law Revue—an annual comedy and musical production—that students can be involved with.

Should you participate in a student organization? During your undergraduate study, you were likely a member of the pre-law society in the hopes it would build your resume and help you get into law school. In reality, participation in such groups probably had little to do with your acceptance into any law school. The same holds true now that you are in law school. Your participation in a student group is unlikely to directly land you the job of your dreams. You should join a student group because you have a genuine interest in that group and because you will meet others with similar interests. You can get to know your classmates and have a forum for socializing. These friends will be useful contacts in your future practice of law. Moreover, they will be your friends, possibly for a lifetime.

C. Faculty/Student and SBA Committees

In addition to student organizations, many schools will permit students to sit on faculty/student committees. Some Committees that are common, include Student Life Committee, Student Enhancement Committee, Admissions Committee, Curriculum Committee, Building Committee, or Library Committee. Some schools will allow students to be involved in faculty appointments and alumni development.

Students also have the opportunity at many schools to participate in the Student Bar Association (or SBA). The duties, structure, and size of the SBA varies among law schools. But for most schools, the SBA is the official student governing body. Through its activities, the SBA advocates student concerns, coordinates student activities and organizations, and is usually charged with appropriating funds for student activities. The SBA Board will usually consist of student representatives from each class (and from different programs, if available at your school). The SBA will have an executive board, that will consist usually of a President, Vice President, Secretary, and Treasurer. Students have a number of opportunities to become involved with the SBA.

D. Public Service and Volunteering

Law school will be a hectic time for you and you will probably feel as if you could not possibly squeeze in any other activities or commitments. Despite that, students should not graduate without some public service or pro bono legal experience. Volunteering for non-profit legal, governmental, or community organizations is valuable opportunity to gain experience and provides students a good opportunity to develop connections in the legal community. Pro bono legal services are done under the supervision of a practicing lawyer, and students may not receive compensation—either pay or academic credit—for doing pro bono work. Public service work is rewarding, helps students develop lawyering skills, teaches students how to work with clients, allows students to gain exposure to various substantive areas of the law, and enhances a resume.

Most schools have a number of options for students who wish to gain experience through public service. Many schools have extensive public service or pro bono programs, or even public interest law centers, dedicated offices, or institutes. Some schools require that students complete a minimum amount of mandatory pro bono (without pay or unit credit) public service before graduating. Only a very small number of schools have no organized public service program.

Schools often provide incentives for students to devote time to public service. Many schools will award scholarships or fellowships for students who wish to assist indigent clients, underrepresented groups, and nonprofit organizations. Part-time and full-time opportunities usually will exist both in the school year and in the summer. Some schools will also fund a limited number of postgraduate public service fellowships. And some schools provide loan-forgiveness for students who intend to enter a public interest law career.

How much public service work should you do? If your goal is to work with a nonprofit or public interest organization after graduation—then quite a bit. These jobs are highly competitive. A career in public interest law typically requires a demonstrated commitment to public interest work. Public interest employers generally want to know that you have a genuine commitment to serving others. Even if you hope to work in the private for-profit sector or in government, you should consider doing a considerable amount of public service work while in law school (maybe 25–75 hours each year). Doing public service activities may be one of the best ways to gain hands-on practical training in law school and is generally valued by employers. Many private law firms are involved in supervising pro bono work, and volunteering can be one of the best ways to meet these attorneys and make connections in the legal community.

———————

Okay, that about covers it. I'm done. Get involved. I'll see you next class."

* * * * *

Well that seemed fairly straightforward. Here's what I had in my notes:

Key Points

☐ Do something, anything—just get involved!

☐ Why? Need to develop practical lawyering skills—improve legal research, writing, analysis, interviewing, counseling, oral advocacy, client interaction etc.

☐ Getting involved may be key to getting a job.

Activities to Consider

☐ Law Review or Law Journal

☐ Externships

☐ Clinical Work

☐ Appellate Advocacy / Moot Court

☐ Trial Advocacy / Mock Trial

☐ Negotiation or Arbitration Programs

☐ Research Assistant

☐ Teaching Assistant

☐ Student Bar Association

☐ Student Organizations and Clubs

☐ Volunteer, Public Service, and Community Organizations

☐ Faculty-Student Committee

☐ The Law Revue (singing and dancing in Law School?) or the Student Newspaper

Chapter 8

Beyond Law School

The first year of law school was not easy, but we had made it. We survived, although some with more scars than others. For me, and my classmates, Professor Lawrence seemed to have inflicted more than his fair share of wounds. I had once heard that law school taught you to think differently. Total understatement. Law school was like a full frontal lobotomy without the anesthesia.

We now turned our minds to the future. What should we do in the summer, and how do we get prepared to enter the "real-world of practice?" Professor Lawrence had a lecture for that too (why was I not surprised). He seemed outright surly this morning as he began to speak.

"The actual practice of law may seem like the horizon to you: you can see it clearly, but it's distant and unapproachable. As far away as it seems now, your plans for the future should be ever in your thoughts. Your time in law school cannot be spent focused solely on class, you must seize opportunities to advance your career goals. Here's some advice. Take it or leave it.

Preparing for Your Career

Keep the end goal in mind. Graduation is not the end zone; you do not spike the ball for the touchdown. You should look beyond Graduation Day with you in a cap and gown, standing next to proud smiling relatives. For most of you, the object of your legal education is to become a practicing attorney. Ultimately, you must find someone who is willing to employ you (for you Mr. James— yes, you in the front row—that's going to be very tough!). And a job search in the legal profession, like other job markets, is an exercise in selling yourself. So look for opportunities throughout law school to make yourself more marketable. You need to start thinking about building a resume and getting practical legal experience after your first year of law school.

Your first year will be an exercise in keeping your head above water. Your focus should be on school and only school in the first year. Once you have closed the book on the last of your first-year exams, however, take a deep breath and get to work planning your sales pitch.

A. Cultivate Relationships

The first step in your marketing campaign is to get some heavy hitters to go to bat for you. You need someone to speak convincingly on your behalf and your professors need to be able to say more than just "Bobby did well in my class, he writes excellent case briefs." When asking a professor for a reference or letter of recommendation, it helps if they can actually pick you out of a crowd. (Yes, Mr. James, unfortunately, I can pick you out of the crowd, but I'm not writing you a letter.)

Recall the words of wisdom I so benevolently bestowed on the importance of developing relationships with your professors. Consider the following scenario: a student walks into my office and says "Professor Lawrence, could you please write me a letter of recommendation? Oh and let me introduce myself, I am John Smith." Both my response and any letter I might write will be lacking in the enthusiasm required to dazzle potential employers.

How can you make contact with your professors? Taking the first step into the magical, mystical, and intimidating world of professors can be daunting for some. It's time to take that leap. Here are several different ways you can begin building those relationships that will lead to references and letters of recommendation.

- *Ask Questions:* Don't have a questions? Make one up, if not about the material, about how the material applies to a particular situation (the question does not have to be brilliant, just not idiotic). If appropriate, ask the professor questions on topics outside of class or about their experiences in the practice of law and share your goals with them. Don't do this once; commit yourself to having a conversation with a professor several times in a semester.

- *Find a Mentor:* By the end of your first year you will inevitably have begun thinking about what kind of law you want to practice. Sit down with professors with expertise in your areas of interest. From speaking with them, you will be able to more accurately define your career goals and get valuable employment advice. Ultimately you will gain a mentor and a reference. You should also consider trying to get connected with alumni, who also may be wonderful mentors.

- *Take Advantage of Academic Writing Opportunities:* In the beginning of your second year, you will likely embark on a fabulous journey (I use the term "fabulous," loosely) into the world of academic writing. Perhaps you will begin this journey through your position on law review. Others will have the opportunity by taking an upper division seminar class. Who best to steer you through the perils and frustrations of publishing an article than those who have gone before you? Many, if not all, of your professors are published academics. Identify a professor, or two or three, who have some expertise on the subject of your article. Build a team of coaches who look at your topic from many different angles and consult with them regularly.

- *Become a Research or Teaching Assistant:* A research assistant or teaching assistant position will allow you to develop a close working relationship with a professor. If you do a good job, you may find someone who can tell future employers about your brilliant analytical mind and the quality of your research and writing skills.

B. Get Practical Experience

Three years from now you will be ready to begin your job search. As you assess your resume you'll be thinking to yourself, hmmm, graduated from law school ... check; passed the bar

exam … check; top of the class, on Law Review, great references.…
check, check, check. Brilliant right? Wrong. The idiosyncrasies of
a legal job search suddenly become apparent. As strange as it might
sound, legal employers expect you have some actual legal experience before you graduate from law school and will not be impressed by how you argued your way out of a traffic ticket. Fortunately, opportunities are abound in law school for you to get the
kind of practical experience employers will expect.

You should not graduate without taking advantage of some of
the opportunities available to you. After you finish your first year,
it's time to dive in to participate in externships, clinics, summer
internships, research and teaching assistant positions, advocacy
programs, and student organizations. Make an effort to add several of these experiences to your resume.

C. Take Advanced Writing/Skills Courses

By the end of your first year of law school you will be rejoicing at
the thought that you can now leave your Legal Writing course behind
you. Think again. As a lawyer you will write constantly and as a new
lawyer it is your writing ability that will make you most valuable to
the partners in your firm. As writing ability is one of the most prized
skills that legal employers value, any honors you receive in a legal
writing course should be included on your resume. Then be sure to
fit an advanced skills course into your schedule before you graduate.
Most law schools offer advanced legal research and writing. Most also
offer appellate advocacy and pretrial practice courses. These kinds of
courses are essential preparations for your ensuing legal career.

D. Meet with the Careers Office

Chances are there is a door you walk by everyday on your way
to class with a sign "Career Service Office" (or something similar).
You've been so busy briefing, outline, studying, panicking and so
on that it has never occurred to you that there might be very smart
people behind that door who know exactly how to get you a job.
Wouldn't it be great to have someone who has been in the busi-

ness for years tell you what to emphasize on your resume to get an employer's attention and what common resume mistakes will send your resume to the trash pile on an employer's desk? It's time to take that leap, cross that threshold and get some expert help. You may not realize all the valuable help and advice waiting for you in this office:

- Resume and cover letter samples
- Tips on how to design and improve your resume
- Help in planning your career goals
- Help in applying for summer internships
- Access to on-line databases with nationwide job postings
- On-campus interviewing opportunities
- Practice interview questions
- Mock interview practice
- Marketing materials sent to out-of-state firms
- Networking opportunities
- Career days and job fairs

The list goes on and on. The career services office is your ambassadors to employment and you must use their expertise. You merely need to want a job badly enough to walk through the door. They will meet you more than half way.

E. Jump at Networking Opportunities

There it is, the "N" word. Networking. You have likely wondered what networking really means and how exactly you are supposed to engage in this well known professional ritual. Let's start with what networking is not. Networking does not mean approaching those you do not know (or have just met) and asking them for a job. It is, simply put, you getting to know other professionals in the legal community. It is a way to build connections that may be helpful to you in the future.

How do you "network?" When you attend an event where other professionals are present, make an attempt to meet attorneys in the community and get to know them. Do not regale them with your many qualifications and in no way expect that your conversations will lead to a job (not at first, at least). This is not an interview, it is a conversation. Be your normal, witty, charming self (unless your normal self is not so charming and witty, in which case pretend this is an interview—in other words, be professional). Enjoy the company of people who share similar interests and who will almost certainly have valuable and insightful thoughts to offer on the practice of law.

I can hear you asking "But doesn't networking mean I rub elbows with influential people, they adore me on the spot for my wit and gumption and give me the corner office?" The popular perception is misleading. It is true that those whom fortune favors may find that a networking opportunity places a job right in their lap. A former student of mine had such an experience. This enterprising student wanted to attend a golf tournament knowing several attorneys in the community were participating. Unfortunately, the cost of the tournament was too steep for a first year law student. Not one to give up easily, the student called up those in charge and arranged to participate for free given his status as a starving law student. At the tournament, he met three attorneys who ultimately offered him a summer clerkship position.

This is the exception, not the rule. Your real hope is that any contacts you make may turn into an opportunity at some point in the future and any effort you make to get to know other professionals in your field will likely pay off in some form. Perhaps you will end up applying at the attorney's firm in the future. Perhaps you will face the attorney as opposing counsel at some point and your relationship will help you reach a favorable settlement. At a minimum, you will likely learn what a law career is like in a certain field and this can help you shape your career goals. You may learn about a field of law you had never thought of before and broaden your career opportunities.

How can you find these all important, much talked of, networking opportunities? Start with events put on by your law school. Your school likely has alumni events where practicing attorneys come back to meet current law students. Really anytime there is an on-campus event which includes practicing attorneys you should make an effort to attend and meet new people. Then look for opportunities outside law school. Your local bar association is a good starting place as they often sponsor events where you are sure to meet other professionals. Finally, think beyond the obvious — follow the example of my student who scored a free ticket to a golf tournament with nothing but initiative.

One last point, just so there is no confusion: networking is not the secret to gainful employment. You are more likely to find a job the traditional way by sending in a resume and interviewing. It is a logical certainty, however, that the more people you know in the legal community, the more likely one of those connections will pan out and assist you in some way in the future.

F. Consider All of Your Options

Some of you came to law school with a specific career plan in mind. You might know you want to practice criminal defense or bankruptcy when you graduate. Most of you have no idea in what area of the law you would like to practice. In making your decision, pay attention to all opportunities available to you. Consider what else is available and evaluate which career best fits your life goals. Maybe you have dreamed of that big firm job making 150k+ a year. Others may have decided to sacrifice salary a little in exchange for a better work-life balance. Either way, most of you, if asked now, would probably anticipate being employed by some type of law firm big or small. In reality there are many options available to you outside of a law firm.

Government Positions: If you haven't already done so, consider practicing as a government attorney. Government positions can be criminal, such as the district attorney's office or public defender's office, or civil, such as the city attorney's office. Opportunities exist at the local (municipal), regional (county), state, and federal level. Don't limit yourself to looking just at your state or local government; consider the abundance of federal jobs available as well. After all, a steady salary, full benefits, great pension and a sense of civic duty make for a great career!

Non-Profit Organizations: Pursue a career in public interest and give back to those in need. If you have not already been in contact with your public interest law society on campus (or public interest center), look them up and ask how you can become involved. Working in the area of public interest is extremely rewarding as you generally help underprivileged or underserved clients in need of an attorney. The Human Rights Project, for example, works to gain asylum for immigrants subject to persecution in their home countries. Legal Aid attorneys generally provide legal services to low-income clients facing eviction, foreclosure, deportation or who are victims of domestic violence. These are just two of many public interest groups working for those who would normally never be able to afford legal assistance. Although many law students become involved in some type of public interest during law school, fewer students actually pursue a career in that area after graduation. Consider doing so. You may not get paid the big bucks, but you will make a salary you can be proud of and you will add meaning to your life and career.

Judicial Clerkships: A judicial clerkship is an opportunity to work in a judge's chambers for usually one or two years immediately following graduation. Judicial clerkships are often fiercely competitive, but if you can land one it will give you an opportunity to work directly with a judge. You will see how a trial works from behind the scenes and have a say in the outcome of the cases you work on. In essence a judicial clerkship allows you to assist in making law. The salary of a judicial clerk may not be comparable to a big-firm salary, but a clerkship only lasts one to two years and it looks great on your resume—making you more marketable when your clerkship is over. Some students only focus on federal district or appellate clerkships. Don't limit yourself. A judicial clerkship with a state court can also be a good experience.

Legal Fellowships: Through a legal fellowship you will learn a specific area of law by practicing for an organization with a particular legal philosophy. The philosophies are diverse: the Christian Legal Fellowship, for instance, offers fellowships with a Christian world view while the ACLU offers fellowships based in a particular political perspective. Fellowships allow you to assume significant responsibility right out of law school and you are usually assigned cutting edge cases. A fellowship usually lasts for one to two years and is a great segue to a future career in a specialized area of law. Your career services office will have information about the various legal fellowships available to you.

Solo Practitioner: Maybe you are a do-it-on-your-own type of person. Many attorneys eventually decide to fly solo and open up their own office. This may prove difficult immediately upon graduation as you will have little practical experience and no established clientele. If a solo career is what you have your heart set on, although challenging, it is not impossible. This is one area where networking will be essential. If you have met sufficient contacts in the legal community, you can get referrals from your new friends. Get as much practical experience in law school as possible. Participate in as many externships as possible. Try a clinic. Take practical skills courses. Keep in mind experience will come with time and so will the clients. A number of good books, websites, and blogs are dedicated to explaining how to start a solo practice. Those resources are good places to start.

In choosing among these (and other) options, try to focus on more than prestige and money. Think about which career path works best for your professional ambitions, and other life goals. Any new graduate has some grunt work to do and must "pay their dues"—you won't be arguing that seminal U.S. Supreme Court case the day after your graduate. But thinking about your long-term goals are important. Are you one who would like to have children and spend time with them? Do you like to travel? Are you willing to move to another city if your employer requires it? Evaluate what your existing commitments are and whether a particular job will allow you to meet them. Evaluate any job offer based on whether it will allow you to be fulfilled in all aspects of your life. Don't be afraid to pursue an entirely different direction than the one in which you may have started out.

Letters of Recommendation

Once you have developed that prized professional relationship with your professor, you will need to ask for the reference or letter of recommendation. When asking for a reference, you must remain personal and professional. Here are some specific tips to keep in mind.

A. Make Good Choices

For almost all recommendation letters you must make good choices on who you ask. Getting an "A" or "A+" in a course is not enough. You must have a recommender who is able to provide thoughtful insights into your intellectual abilities, and usually your writing, research, and analytical skills. The best letters often are able to address your ability to critically analyze complete facts and legal doctrines, as well as your ability to articulate cogent and effective legal arguments. Better yet, you want a recommendation letter that comments on your personal traits—these kinds of letters often sound more genuine and persuasive. You only want recommendation letters from professors who can provide a strong recommendation. If you sense reluctance on the part of the professor, ask someone else.

B. Approach Recommenders Directly

Personal conversations are much better than impersonal e-mails when asking for a recommendation letter. Furthermore, think of whether meeting in person with you professor is the better choice for communications prior to asking for a letter of recommendation. Use e-mails only for quick questions with short answers. They do not count towards your goal of building a relationship with your professor. Be professional in all your communications with your professors, e-mail and in person. You are building your professional reputation from your first day in law school. Your professionalism, or lack thereof, is something that your professors will certainly comment on in any letter of recommendation and something that every employer will consider.

C. Ask, Don't Presume

Make sure when you ask for a reference or letter of recommendation, you do just that—ASK! Never presume. Don't notify me that you have put me down as a reference. Ask me if I am willing to serve as a reference (or else you might not appreciate what I have to say when your employer calls). Ask in person! Asking for a reference or letter of recommendation in person is a way to re-connect with your professor and keep the relationship that you have been working on fresh in their minds. It is also much more personal and professional to see your professor and ask for the courtesy in person.

D. Give Plenty of Notice

Professors are busy. When asking for a letter of recommendation, give your professors plenty of advance notice to write the letter. If you walk into my office and tell me that you need a letter by the week's end, it will be easy for me to assume that you believe the world revolves around you and that you have little respect for my time or other professional commitments. Give me at least two weeks notice (if not more), whenever possible. Providing plenty of notice increases not only the chance that I will write the letter, but also the chance the letter will be one of quality.

E. Make It Easy for the Recommender

Unless the letter is to be submitted electronically, provide your professor with a filled-out, pre-addressed, stamped envelope (unless the recommender asks for something different). Make things easy for the recommender to send the letter. Be sure to provide the address where the letter must be sent, and any forms that need to be included with the letter. If there are forms that need to be completed, complete the basic information that needs to be filled out about you and the recommender's contact information. Most importantly, be sure to provide the deadline for the letter.

F. Provide Detailed Information

Don't presume your professors know you as well as you do. Even if your recommender knows you well, they may not remember every bit of your life-story that could be helpful in writing a

letter. Provide your recommenders, at the very least: (1) your resume; (2) your unofficial transcript; (3) your personal statement
(if one is required for the application); and (4) if appropriate, a
copy of your best work for the professor or a summary of your
work and other accomplishments. Remind your professor of any
specific details that might be helpful in writing the letter (e.g., you
scored the top grade in the class, you received an award for your
performance, etc.). This will give the writer a better opportunity
to comment thoroughly on your abilities and qualifications.

Consider providing the recommender this information in both
hard copy and electronic form. Be sure to tell your recommenders
all the places you are applying, and try not to blindside them with
seriatim requests for additional letters. Providing a full list of the
programs and places you are applying at once is much easier than
having to send out many letters in small batches.

G. Remember to Follow Up

Let your recommenders know what happens. Also, sometimes
letters get lost or professors forget to write them. Double-check
that your letter arrived. And be sure to thank the recommender
with a short thank you card or note.

The Summer Clerkship

So you landed that summer clerkship that has made you the envy
of all your friends and there you are in a newly dry-cleaned suit
with your designer briefcase off to your first day on the job. Nervous, probably, because you don't know what is expected of you. No
fear, you are sure to outshine all other law clerks, past, present, and
future if you can remember the following very basic tips:

A. Act Professionally

Remember, you are there to make an impression. Perhaps you
are hoping for a full time job. At the minimum you will need your

employer to serve as a reference. To make the right impression, you need to display professional behavior throughout the entire clerkship.

Show up on time—every day and for everything. If you are asked to be at the office at 8:00 a.m., your supervising attorney will expect to see you there at 8:00 a.m. Not 8:05. Not 8:15. In fact, your supervising attorney will likely walk by your office at 8:00 a.m. just to see if you are there. Shock them—show up at 7:45! Traffic and your alarm not going off are not good excuses for being late. If a meeting begins at 11:00 a.m., you better be sure to be there before it starts. You can't afford to be late.

Be genuinely friendly and nice to everyone in the firm. You need to be respectful to not just the partners or associates at the firm, but the secretaries, paralegals, law librarians, security guards, and other staff. The staff will be asked their opinion of you by the hiring partners so make sure they like you. Be respectful to other summer clerks as well. They may turn out to be your colleagues in the future.

A related point: be modest. No matter how smart you think you are, you know almost nothing about practicing law. So, for the sake of your own career, don't pretend that you do. Firms don't like summer clerks who are pretentious, and they won't offer them jobs after graduation.

B. Dress Professionally

Be sure to dress as others do in the office and err on the side of being conservative (okay, boring) in how you dress. Most of the time for most law offices, you should wear a dark suit, a white shirt or blouse, and, if a man, a conservative tie. This is not the time for lime green shirts, Technicolor-swirl ties, and light-colored, five-button down blazers—found only on fashion runways. If there's a casual Friday, don't be too casual. Again, be conservative. Don't wear anything too flashy or sexy, and keep the jewelry to a minimum. This is not the time to show-off your multiple piercings and tattoos.

C. Submit Assignments on Time

Turn all assignments in on time. If you are given a deadline and you will not be able to make it, tell your supervising attorney at the time you are given the assignment. Yes, it is okay to tell a supervising attorney that you have too many deadlines to complete their project in time. That is, if you really do have that much work. Telling your supervising attorney you cannot meet a deadline because of a baseball game or a baby shower will not bode well. If you discover after you receive an assignment that you will not be able to finish the project in time, tell your supervising attorney at the moment you realize that you cannot make the deadline— never wait until the deadline to let them know it is not finished. Never let the deadline pass without turning in the assignment or speaking with your supervisor.

D. Always Bring Pen and Paper

Show up to meetings with a pen and a legal pad or notebook. Anytime an attorney asks you to come to their office or attend a meeting, you will likely need to take notes. You will not be able to remember everything your supervising attorney tells you and you appear unprofessional to presume that you can. So have a stack of notebooks ready and always grab one on your way in to talk to an attorney.

E. Ask Appropriate Questions

As law students, you are not expected to know everything. Your employer will know this is your first legal experience and you are just getting your feet wet. Although they will not expect you to know everything, they will expect you to ask questions when you are unclear on the assignment or task. You must ensure that you understand every assignment you are given.

Ask questions to clarify exactly what end product your supervisor is expecting. Does she want oral feedback on your research?

Does he want a written product, such as an office memorandum? Does your supervisor want you to actually draft a brief or motion? Ask question to clarify how much time you should spend on a project. Perhaps your supervisor thinks the project can be done in 10 hours. You don't want to come back to your supervisor with the project after having billed 20 hours.

Ask questions as you are completing and after you have completed the project. You should never guess what to do. If you do not know an answer, simply take the time to walk down to the attorneys office, tell them what you have, and ask your question. Bring what you have completed with you. At some point, you also want to ask for feedback. Only with feedback will you be able to improve, and most supervisors want to see new attorneys (no matter how green) excel and succeed.

F. Work Hard

Your clerkship is your opportunity to impress practicing attorneys and to learn. There is a chance that your summer job will lead to an offer of full time employment. Some summer clerkships often give the appearance that you are there merely to be catered to and enjoy yourself. If you are clerking for a large firm with a "summer program," you will likely be taken to the spa, golfing, sports games, etc. Don't let these fun activities mislead you. You are there to work and make a good impression. Even if it appears the firm does not expect you to work hard, work hard. Work very hard. They are watching to see who will step up to the plate.

When I say work hard, however, you want to keep standard hours. If most associates are arriving at 8:30 a.m. and leaving at 6:30 p.m., you should too. You don't want to be eccentric. Don't keep strange hours (like beginning at 11 a.m. and working until midnight). The people you work with will not be impressed and will start wondering why you are taking so much longer than others getting your work finished.

G. Proof Read. Proof Read. Proof Read.

Did I say that enough times? I can't overemphasize how important it is. Good attorneys are meticulous, perhaps even to a fault. Your work product means little if it is smothered with spelling mistakes, grammar errors, and other symptoms of poor writing (e.g., excessive use of passive voice, nominalizations, long-winded sentences, etc.). Actually, any kind of typo can undermine your credibility. You want to turn in work product—even when the partner asks for a draft—that is professionally formatted, has no typos or grammatical errors, and is written in a clear, easy-to-read, writing style. Equally unhelpful is a memo or brief that relies on bad law. Make sure to shepardize all your cases and cite-check carefully. Appearance is more than half the game.

A related point. Quality of work is usually always more important than quantity. If it takes you a month to write a four-page memo, you're in trouble. But summer clerks are almost always evaluated on the quality of the work they submit and not the sheer amount of work completed. Make each project count.

H. Go to Firm Functions

As mentioned, your summer employer may have special functions for the summer clerks: dinner or wine tasting, a baseball game, white water rafting trips, a round of golf, or a spa day. I know what you are thinking—no one will have to twist your arms to get you there! When you start your summer clerkship and realize your firm has an event every evening, sheer exhaustion may tempt you to skip the ones that are less interesting you. Don't. Your employer will spend the summer evaluating not just your work product but how well you fit into the firm, not to mention your commitment and stamina. They expect you to go to all the functions unless you have a darn good reason to miss (completing a work assignment on time is a good reason). Show up, smile, and act like you are having the time of your life even if you are tired of spending every evening with the same people you see all day at work. Going to firm events shows an interest in the firm.

Don't be fooled, the firm functions and events are part of your summer-long interview for this job. Treat the events like interviews. No matter how casual the event—and even if partners and associates are acting outrageously—you are under constant evaluation. Don't blow it. For many employers, social events are intended to see how you interact with other people. This doesn't mean you shouldn't enjoy yourself. But don't let your hair down too much. This is not the time to be revealing past indiscretions or any other personal thing about you that may reflect badly. You must continue to act professionally.

Some obvious points, but perhaps worth emphasizing. If you drink, drink in moderation (moderation at most firms is one or possibly two drinks in an evening). Never get buzzed at a firm event. Also, don't try to date or sleep with partners, partners' spouses, associates, or summer associates. I'm not going into more detail. It's a bad idea, and if you don't know why then you don't deserve to be a lawyer. And a last obvious point—never tell off-color jokes.

I. Take Advantage of Firm Training

Many private law firms will offer summer clerks some training workshops. It may be a deposition workshop, or a writing workshop, or a session on client development. Take advantage of any training programs or workshops offered. They usually provide you important insight into what the firm expects of you, and also provides you with an opportunity to get to know (and possibly impress) more firm associates and partners. Failing to attend these training workshops may suggest that you're not sufficiently interested in the firm.

After Graduation

The first year of practice may be overwhelming regardless of which career path you choose. You will be learning a whole new area of law or trying to quickly absorb the intricacies and nuances of one you thought you had learned in law school. Unlike in law school, you now have real clients who depend upon your competence. Here are some important things to keep in mind as you make this transition and begin your career.

A. Build a Professional Reputation

Judges talk. Lawyers talk. They especially love to talk about other attorneys. Sometimes they talk about new attorneys who have impressed them. Usually they spend their time talking about the humorous and inappropriate behavior displayed by unprofessional attorneys. Anytime you think it is not important to be on time, or to dress professionally, or to make strong arguments in support of your position, think about the judges and senior attorneys sitting around at lunch laughing at you. Think about how your actions will spread throughout the legal community and affect your career.

The manner in which you conduct yourself in the courtroom or in a negotiation will soon be known to all. Within your first year of practice (even within the first few months) you will have established a reputation for what type of lawyer you are. Think now about what you want that reputation to be. Will you be a professional who behaves respectfully to judges, opposing attorneys, and court personnel? Will you be known as a thoughtful, hard working attorney who takes the time to develop strong arguments supported by law? Will you be known as intellectually honest? Will judges know you as someone whose written briefs are designed to persuade but not mislead and which never leave out important case law that supports the other side? Will you be known as someone who manages their time well in order to get all assignments done on time and not at the last minute? Perhaps most importantly, are you someone who practices law with integrity and unimpeachable ethics or do you practice using shady tactics skirting the ethics laws just shy of breaking them?

How you dress and speak, the quality of your work product, and how you treat others is critical to your success as an attorney. This is not to say that you can never make a mistake. You will make mistakes. Count on it. Your character is revealed by how you deal with the mistakes. New lawyers tend to try to hide the mistake and hope it goes away. This can only end badly for your client and your career. Good attorneys go immediately to their supervisor and get help fixing the mistake. Good lawyers never make the same mistake again.

B. Join Local Bar Associations

In most states a large number of local bar associations exist. Some are organized geographically (e.g., the Beverly Hills Bar Association, Santa Monica Bar Association, and the Glendale Bar Association), others are organized by personal characteristics (e.g., the Black Women Lawyer's Bar Association, Lesbian & Gay Bar Association, and the Iranian-American Bar Association), and some are organized by practice area (e.g., the Los Angeles Intellectual Property Law Association, the Labor & Employment Law Section of the Los Angeles County Bar Association, and the Individual Rights Section of the Los Angeles County Bar Association). Local and specialty bar associations are in some ways social clubs where you can network, meet new friends, and learn about the substantive area of law and your business. Whether you are a sole practitioner, a partner in a small firm, or are working for a giant mega-firm, networking is important to build your law practice and increase your visibility in the profession. Joining a bar association is a good way to do that. Most Bar Associations will have mixers and continuing legal education events throughout the year.

C. Keep in Contact

Once you become a practicing lawyer, don't close the book on law school. It is imperative that you maintain your law school relationships after law school as they will be valuable to you in the future.

Let's start with your law school friends. Imagine this. You are working at a mid-sized firm following graduation and things seem to be going well. Then the senior partner in the firm walks in your office and starts talking to you about partnership and the requirement that you start bringing in clients. Where are you going to find the clients? Well, if you have kept in touch with everyone in law school, you will have a source of attorneys who can refer clients to you that their firm is not able to serve. Or, imagine your senior partner came to tell you the firm is merging and you may need to find a new job. Wouldn't it be nice if you kept in touch with those who may have an opening at their firm?

Now let's talk about those important law school professors. Perhaps you are working as a judicial clerk and your clerkship ends. You now need a new job and that job requires references. Wouldn't you like to know you have kept in touch with your professors so you can easily call them up and ask them to be a reference? The longer it has been since you spoke to that professor, the more difficult it will be to ask them to be a reference. So keep in touch over the years in one fashion or another.

One way to keep in touch is to go back to your law school and volunteer. Most law schools need judges for moot court or have alumni events where you can reconnect with old professors and classmates. As an alum, you have a responsibility to go back and help your school. It just happens that this is also a good way to maintain relationships that will be rewarding to you and helpful to you on a professional level.

D. Remain Flexible in Your Career

Hopefully when you graduate you will have a job lined up and you will love it. Unfortunately, the majority of you will not yet have found your dream job. Perhaps you even have a job lined up and you think it is the dream job. You may discover your boss is a nightmare or that you can't possibly practice that type of law for the rest of your life. No worries. Things change. Remain flexible. Keep your eye out. You are never stuck in a job you don't enjoy. Find that job that makes you want to get up in the morning and go to work. Find the job that makes you proud to be a lawyer. And never give up looking for it until it is yours.

That's all for today. I'm done.

* * * * *

As with other lectures of Prof. Lawrence, I took some selected notes. Here's what I had.

The Basics

- ☐ Cultivate relationships with professors while at law school (at some point will need recommendation letters)
- ☐ Get as much practical hands-on experience as possible (think externships, clinics, summer jobs)
- ☐ Make alumni connections and network
- ☐ Take advanced writing courses in second and third years (the more the better)
- ☐ Enroll in advanced skill and capstone courses
- ☐ Take advantage of the Career Services Office and plan a job-search strategy

Letters of Recommendation

- ☐ Ask only people (professors) I know well
- ☐ Ask in person for a letter of recommendation (not by e-mail or phone)
- ☐ Ask before using someone as a reference
- ☐ Give plenty of notice for professors to write a letter of recommendation (2 weeks minimum)
- ☐ Provide pre-addressed, stamped envelope to recommender
- ☐ Provide detailed information about self (resume, transcript, copy of best work etc.)
- ☐ Follow up
- ☐ Send thank you notes to recommenders

The Summer Job

- ☐ Act professionally and be friendly to everyone
- ☐ Dress conservatively and professionally
- ☐ Always bring pen and paper when meeting with supervisors

☐ Be clear as to expectations and what supervisor/client wants before beginning project

☐ Always submit assignments on time

☐ Be extra-meticulous with all written work product (proofread to ensure no typos or errors)—there's no such thing as a draft!

☐ Actively seek out feedback

☐ Go to firm functions and get to know supervisors, partners and other attorneys

☐ Treat all events as interviews

☐ Work hard—you've got one chance!

After Graduation

☐ Reputation is everything!

☐ Join local bar and community organizations

☐ Continue to network with law school alumni (get a mentor!)

☐ Stay in contact with classmates

☐ Stay in contact with your school

☐ Keep your eye out for opportunities

Chapter 9

The Bar Exam

What? It couldn't be. But sure enough it was. There, standing at the front of the bar review class, was Professor Lawrence. After a summer course and then brutal first year with this joker, I thought I was done with him. Had he not belittled and tortured us enough? Yet here he was again. He didn't seem to have gotten any younger, friendlier, or prettier in the last two years.

"Well, let me say it. I'm stunned. I would have thought you lot would have been kicked out of school long ago. Hard to believe you made it. You've probably had soft professors over the last two years. Well stop slacking, it's time to kick it up a gear. You have one last hurdle—to pass the bar exam. Some students become excessively worried about the exam. You shouldn't be. If you passed my class, the bar exam is a stroll in a park. Anyone can pass, if they approach the exam correctly. Here's how.

Preparing for the Bar Exam

Too many graduating law students fail to properly prepare for the bar exam. Many take the exam seriously, but some students each year appear to believe the exam is overly easy. While it's not a complicated exam, it does require lots of preparation. After all of the work and stress of law school, the bar exam is not the time to let up.

A. Have the Right Mindset

You can pass the bar exam on your first attempt, but you must approach preparing for the exam with the right mindset. First, you must take it seriously. Passing a bar exam is as much about commitment as it is about learning substantive law. Never take a Bar Exam for "practice" or as a "trial run." Sitting for the exam with the intent to take it again will become a self-fulfilling prophecy. You must commit to working hard and passing the exam the first time. Second, you need to approach the exam with a positive attitude, knowing you will pass if you prepare properly. The exam is difficult, but it's not rocket science. Students who have earned a JD from an accredited school have the skills necessary to pass the exam the first time. That's true even for the most notoriously difficult bar exams: California's and New York's.

B. Focus in Law School

The best preparation for the bar exam occurs in law school. For most law schools there exists a strong correlation between class rank and bar pass rate. Students who do well in law school pass at higher rates than students who have performed poorly. This does not mean that students with low GPAs will fail the bar exam. But they are at a greater risk. So engaging and doing your best in law school is a good way to get prepared for the bar exam.

This does not mean that you must take every course in law school that covers a bar-related topic. Studies have shown very little, if any, correlation between the substantive material studied in law school and bar exam performance. Instead, be certain to enroll in rigorous courses that force you to write, to think analytically, and to master complicated legal issues. You do not want to take a course that you have no interest in solely because that topic is tested on the exam. Take courses that will challenge you and that will improve your writing and analytical skills.

Another reason exists to take rigorous courses that focus on legal analysis. Commercial bar preparation courses that you take while studying for the bar exam often will not teach you how to write an exam essay or do legal analysis. Preparation courses will usually teach you the black-letter law of the topics tested comprehensively, but those courses provide very little in the way of how to write, or how to analyze—you are assumed to have learned those skills in law school.

Many schools now have a variety of programs and workshops that are designed to help you pass the exam your first time. The ABA now permits law schools to offer bar preparation courses for credit. If your school offers those programs, you should take advantage of them.

C. Understand the Exam Structure

Each state has different exam requirements, but most exams are roughly similar. Typically, a bar exam will be two days, with a few states having three-day exams. One day is devoted to multiple choice questions, and the other days are devoted to different kinds of essays. Some states have short essays, others long, and some states have small sets of multiple choice questions related to specific topics of law. Some states, such as California, also use performance exams.

Each day of the bar exam usually involves six hours of testing (three hours in the morning, three hours in the afternoon). With the exception of a few states, the Multistate Bar Exam (MBE) occupies one full day. The MBE portion of the exam consists of 200 multiple choice questions on the following subjects: contracts, torts, constitutional law, criminal law and procedure, evidence, and real property.

Most states will also require that students complete a day of essay exams. Some states, however, also utilize a performance exam. A performance exam is designed to be a realistic situation that an attorney might encounter early in their career. For each question, the applicant receives a case file and a library (a collection of statutes and cases). The applicant is then assigned a task, such as writing an opinion letter, a brief, a memo, or a closing argument.

In addition to the bar exam itself, many states require that candidates pass the Multistate Professional Responsibility Exam (MPRE) before being admitted to practice. The MPRE is a two hour and five minute exam, consisting of sixty multiple choice questions. The exam is administered three times a year in March,

August, and November. Generally, students should take the MPRE well in advance of the bar exam.

D. Meet Deadlines

Each state has its own requirements. Before a student's last year in law school—as much as twelve to fourteen months before graduation—students should know what they must do to become licensed in the state in which they intend to practice. Each state has their own requirements (including, among other things, registering, as well as submitting an application, fingerprint cards, and a moral character petition, etc.). Fortunately, most states have web sites that provide detailed information about the requirements to practice law.

You should pay close attention to deadlines. The application process can be expensive (often several hundred dollars), and submitting a late application will increase the fees significantly. In several states a late application fee can nearly double the cost of the application. You also need to be careful not to miss deadlines to submit requests to type the exam on your laptop or for disability accommodations. For most states, the bar application is due several months before a student graduates. Many states also require that students meet certain "moral character and fitness" requirements. This process may require letters of reference and possibly interviews. Although requirements vary among jurisdictions, you must ensure that you complete all required paperwork on time.

E. Prepare Financially

The bar exam is expensive. The costs of submitting an application and completing a preparation course will for many jurisdictions approach or exceed $5,000. Graduating students often borrow money to finance the costs of bar exam registration, exam-related preparatory materials, and the living expenses during the two months from graduation to the date of the exam. This is known as a "bridge" or "bar" loan. Most financial aid offices have information for students about sources of funding for bridge loans. At the start of your last year of law school, make an appointment with a financial aid counselor at your school to see what options may be available to you.

You should do your best to get your finances in order so that you do not have to work while studying for the exam. Studying for the exam is a full-time job. For many exams—like the California and New York exams—working while studying for the exam is a bad decision and will significantly increase you chances of failure. If you do need to work while preparing for the exam, you should have a frank discussion with your employer about what time you will need off to study. In California, for example, working any significant amount is almost certain to lead to exam failure.

This is also not the time to shy away from a loan. Taking out a bar study loan and studying full-time is much cheaper than working while studying and then failing. Not passing on your first attempt means at least six more months of not being an attorney, as well as incurring the costs of having to pay another bar registration fee and take another bar preparation course.

F. Research Preparation Courses

In your last year of law school (or perhaps earlier), you should carefully research and determine which commercial bar review/bar preparation course you will be taking. Taking a commercial preparation course is not optional. For almost all jurisdictions it's essential to passing the bar exam. You will take a preparation course if you plan to pass.

You want to weigh a number of factors before deciding on a bar preparation course. For different courses ask yourself, what is the cost? How often do the classes meet? Who teaches the course? How is instruction provided? How is feedback provided and how does the course assess your progress? Is the course comprehensive? What is the success rate for students taking the course? Does the course's approach fit your learning style? There are many good commercial preparation courses, but there also some very poor ones. Be sure to do the research ahead of time so that you feel comfortable with the decision you've made. Talk to other (hopefully friends you trust) who have recently taken the course. Get a sense of what they liked and disliked.

The courses are expensive—usually several thousands of dollars—so you want to ensure you've done your research. Be wary of courses that cost several thousand dollars more than other courses in your jurisdiction. If a commercial bar preparation course promises something that sounds too good to be true, it probably is.

G. Clear the Decks

From the time you graduate until you take the bar exam—for most states and schools approximately two months—you need to study ten or more hours a day, at least six days a week. To focus solely on the exam during those two months, you must get your life in order. Stock up on any regular medications you need, so that you do not run out. Take care of any errands that you would otherwise do (e.g., getting your car fixed, seeing the dentist or the doctor, taking your pet to the vet). Consider pre-paying any bills that will become due during the study period. Remove as many distractions from your life as possible.

Tell your family and friends how important this exam is. You must explain that you will be mostly unavailable for the two months leading up to the exam. The two months that you are studying for the exam is also not the time to be making any major changes in your life. This is not the time to have surgery, take a vacation, get married or divorced, move homes, or start a new relationship.

If you are a parent, also plan for your children. If you have young children, be certain to arrange for child care and back-up child care. And for your children, factor time to spend with your children into your study schedule. You need to study, but family is important too.

H. Petition for Accommodations

Most states provide reasonable accommodations for applicants with documented disabilities. If you have received special accommodations for exams during law schools, you should attempt to get those same accommodations for the bar exam. Each jurisdiction, however, has its own procedures for determining whether an applicant is permitted exam accommodations. If you have a physical or learning disability be certain to submit the testing accommodation forms early. You must also ensure that you have sufficient documentation to support the accommodation.

Studying for the Bar Exam

Not only is it important that you prepare for the bar exam, but during the approximately two months between graduation and the exam you must study properly. Here's how:

A. Take a Preparation Course

Commercial bar preparation courses are a must. They are not optional. You need to take one to pass the bar exam. There are many good courses out there, with many different teaching styles. Pick one.

Once you have picked one, be sure to do exactly what they tell you and follow their study plans. Be sure to follow the advice they give precisely. If they tell you to take a practice exam, you take a practice exam. If they tell you to read an outline, read the outline. If they tell you to write 50 MBE (multiple choice) questions a day, write 50 MBE questions a day. You are paying a lot of money to have them help you pass the exam. You should follow their advice exactly.

B. Create a Schedule

To pass most bar exams you must learn and memorize a large number of rules, take many practice exams, and attend bar review courses. You need to plan for how you will get it all done. Schedule what you will do every day for each week. The schedule should be detailed, indicating exactly when you will attend your bar preparation course and listen to lectures, when you will take practice exams, when you'll practice MBE questions, and when you will review your notes and outlines. Generally you should get up early and do your most difficult studying first. You should schedule in time to exercise, take breaks, and eat. You will need to take a periodic evening or afternoon off, and may need to schedule time to spend with your spouse, children or other loved ones. Schedule it all. Stick to your schedule.

C. Study Ten to Twelve Hours a Day

Each jurisdiction is different, and the difficulty of the exams vary widely. But as a rule of thumb, studying for the bar exam require studying ten to twelve hours each day, five or six days a week. For most bar exams, the amount of material you need to learn during the two months leading up to the exam is voluminous. To master all the material and take sufficient practice exams requires studying full time. This means for most exams you should plan on studying ten to twelve hours a day or more. When studying, be sure to work steadily.

D. Study Actively, Not Passively

You will not pass the bar exam if you spend all your time memorizing outlines, flashcards, or notes. If you devote all your study time to reviewing notes and memorizing rules, you increase your chance of failure. You need to practice the questions to learn how the rules you are memorizing work in practice. Only by writing practice questions will you train yourself to spot issues.

Said differently, you must learn actively. You should take literally thousands of MBE practice questions, and write out many practice essay exams. As a general rule, you should answer at least 50 practice MBE a day and write several sample essay exams each day. So students will do as many as 100 MBE multiple-choice questions a day. Importantly, do not wait until you know the black-letter law to take practice exams. Instead, taking the practice exams is a way for you to learn the law. When you take a practice exam, it's important that you assess how you're doing. Be sure to review your answer carefully and analyze what you did well and what you need to improve on.

E. Take Timed Practice Exams

Equally important as taking practice exams is to take some of those exams timed. It's one thing to write an answer to an essay exam, or to answer 100 multiple choice questions. It's quite another thing to do it within the time constraints imposed by the bar. You must take practice exams in "real life conditions." Taking timed exams is also critical for another reason: it builds your confidence. Your bar preparation course should give you dozens of practice questions. Many states provide sample questions on their state bar webpages. And in many law school libraries you can find books that contain past exams or sample questions. Take several timed-practice essay exams each week. After you have taken the exam, be certain to assess how you did.

F. Manage Your Environment

When studying for the bar exam or taking practice exams ensure that you are in a comfortable place without distractions. Ideally you should be in a place where you have enough room to stretch out: where you can place your outlines, and notes, and bar review materials. Before beginning think ahead so you have what you need for the next hour. You don't want to be jumping up every few minutes to get a book, or a pen, or another cup of coffee. You also want to ensure you're not too close to friends. The bar exam is not the time to be catching up on the latest gossip. You have to focus on concentrated studying.

G. Stay Healthy

Managing stress and reducing anxiety is critical for doing well. When you're stressed you do not retain and remember the material you're studying, and studying becomes inefficient. Exercise is a valuable way to reduce stress. So too is staying healthy by eating good food on a regular basis. Stay away from alcohol, tobacco and excessive amounts of caffeine during the months you're studying for the bar (although, this is not the time to quit one's bad habits). Get plenty of sleep. In short, use common sense and stay as healthy as you can.

Answering Bar Exam Questions

How do you answer a bar exam essay question? Usually the same way you answered law school exam essay questions. Here's a reminder of the key points:

A. Use IRAC

To pass the bar exam, you must demonstrate your ability to use legal analysis and organize your answer. When answering questions on the bar exam, use IRAC—Issue, Rule, Analysis/Application, Conclusion. For each question asked, spot the relevant issues, explain what rules relate to those issues, use the facts that are relevant to the issues, and draw a reasoned conclusion. You must make a logical and reasoned argument that explains why the facts show that certain elements or rules have been met or not met. Remember, applying the facts does not mean simply restating the facts or regurgitating the question. Do not assume that the reader knows any of the facts. You must show your work, and explain your thought process in a logical way.

You want the bar exam grader to understand your analysis easily and quickly. Consider writing each part of the IRAC as a separate paragraph. Here's a sample answer to a bar exam evidence essay question, with each part of the IRAC labeled.

A. Is Paul's Statement "I Shot Him" Inadmissible Hearsay [**Issue**]

Hearsay is an out-of-court statement used to prove the truth of the matter asserted. Hearsay is inadmissible unless an exception to the hearsay rule applies. [**Rule**]

In this case, the facts say Paul said "I shot him" at the nightclub. Because the statement was made in a nightclub and not in a court room under oath, it's an out-of-court statement. The prosecutor is trying to establish that Paul is guilty of murder for killing John, the victim, who died from a gunshot wound. The statement "I shot him" is therefore being used to prove that Paul in fact shot John rather than for some other purpose. [**Analysis**]

Because both elements of hearsay are met, Paul's statement is hearsay and would be inadmissible unless an exception applies. [**Conclusion**]

Notice how the heading serves as the "I" of the IRAC. The rule, analysis, and conclusion section of the IRAC is identified as a separate paragraph. Breaking the analysis up this way makes the answer easy to read and grade.

B. Allocate Your Time

Just as with law school exams, allocating your time is critical. If the bar exam gives you three hours to write three essays, you must spend no more than one hour on each essay. The reason for this is simple: you must pass all the portions of the exam. Doing very well on one essay question, and very poorly on another question will lead to a failing grade. As soon as your allocated time has expired—even if you're not finished with your answer—you must move on to the next question. If you have time left over at the end of the exam, you can go back to earlier questions.

C. Use Headings and Subheadings

Bar examiners are busy. They are tired. They spend less than a few minutes reading each exam and they've read literally thousands of poorly written exams. They don't have time to hunt out difficult to find arguments and analysis. You must make it as easy as possible for the grader to recognize that you have spotted the correct legal issues and answered the question asked. To do this, use headings and subheadings that are easily distinguished from the text. Identify every main issue that the exam raises with a heading. Use subheadings to separate sub-issues, elements, or factors.

But don't misunderstand this advice. Headings and subheadings are appropriate, but avoid sub-sub-headings and sub-sub-sub headings. A bar exam answer is not an outline. You want to make it easy for the reader to understand your analysis; too many subdivisions is distracting.

D. Approach the Exam Methodically

As with law school exams, you should approach the essay question methodically. First, read the call of the question. What is the question asking? What area of the law is implicated? Second, read the question carefully. And then read it again. Make note of the important facts. Third, outline—in brief form—your answer. Do not start writing until you have thought through what main issues are implicated by the question and how you intend to organize your answer. Fourth, start writing your answer. As explained above, be sure to stop writing and move on once the time you've allocated for the question is up.

E. Use the Word *Because*

As with law school exams, it's critical that you explain how you reach your conclusions. A conclusion without a reason is not a passing bar exam. Use the word *because* to show why the facts of the problem show that legal rules are met or not met. To pass the bar exam, you must demonstrate that you understand how to apply legal concepts in particular factual circumstances to reach a probable conclusion.

F. Argue Both Sides

For many (but not all) of the issues raised by a bar exam question, you must explain what the strongest arguments for both sides are. If you think the plaintiff will win, what is the strongest argument for the defendant? If you think a legal element is met, what is the strongest argument that it is not met? Be sure to highlight to bar examiners when the questions asked are "close calls." Explain the differing arguments that could be made, and then explain why you think one side of the argument will prevail over the other.

Some Practicalities

Doing well on the bar exam requires mastering anxiety and ensuring that you are not distracted during the exam period. To help with managing stress and anxiety and give yourself the best chances of succeeding, consider doing the following:

A. Reserve a Hotel Room

Do not commute long distances to the bar exam. Be certain to book a hotel room near the examination site (close enough to walk to and from the hotel). Rooms often fill-up quickly near exam sites, so book early. As soon as you find out where you are taking the exam, make a reservation. Avoid sharing rooms with others: you need a quite place to unwind each night of the exam.

If you are unable to stay in a hotel during the exam or would prefer to stay at home, be certain to know ahead of time how to get to the exam site, and where to park if you are driving. If you are commuting, do a dry run during rush hour so you know exactly how long it will take to get to the exam site. If you are commuting, be sure to leave early. If you are driving, you might consider carpooling (or, at least have a back-up if something happens to your car).

B. Tie-Up Loose Ends

Think ahead. If you have children, be certain that you have arranged for child care. If you have pets, make sure you have someone who can look after them during the two or three days of the exam. If you are taking the exam using a laptop, ensure that your laptop is working properly. Pack the supplies you will take to the exam ahead of time (such as pens, pencils, highlighters, aspirin, a timer, etc.).

C. Visit the Exam Site

You do not want to be worrying about where you need to go on the day of the exam. Visit where you are taking the exam long before exam day. Make sure you know where you're going and how to get there.

D. Pack Ahead of Time

The day or night before the bar exam is not the time to pack. Be sure to pack ahead of time so that you don't forget anything you need. If the exam permits a silent timer, do you have one? An alarm clock that works? Your laptop? Have you packed sufficient pens, pencils, and highlighters? Do you have comfortable clothes? Perhaps you might even pack snacks. Think through what you need and pack ahead of time. Also, to prevent unpleasant surprises, read the exams instruction very carefully so you know exactly what is permitted in the exam room.

The Day of the Bar Exam

Not only should you prepare ahead of time, you should keep in mind what you will need on the first day of the exam.

A. Wear Comfortable Clothes

A bar exam is not a fashion show. Don't worry about how you look. Nobody cares at the bar exam. Wear your most comfortable clothes, and wear them in layers. The air conditioning or heating may be blasting, or not working at all. Layers will allow you to respond to any conditions.

B. Eat Breakfast, Lunch and Dinner

Be sure to eat during breaks in the exam. For breakfast you do not want something heavy—this is not time for the lumberjacks special with a double-extra side of sausage and bacon—but it will be a long day and you need to eat something.

Plan ahead. For some exam testing centers in large cities, there may be hundreds of students taking the exam at the same time. In those cases, it may be difficult to eat at a nearby restaurant during the allocated lunch break. Consider packing lunch. It may save you some unnecessary stress and put you in a better position for the afternoon portion of the exam.

C. Arrive Early

Much of the key to passing the bar exam is managing stress. You cannot do well on the exam if you panic. To reduce stress, be sure to arrive early. Check-in. Get a good seat (if the examiners don't assign one to you). Get focused. You will not be permitted to take the exam if you arrive late. So don't make it close. Get to the exam site with plenty of time to spare.

D. Leave Your Study Materials

You can not cram for the bar exam. Doing so is a waste of time. Do not bother trying to learn anything new right before the exam. You'll just stress yourself. So leave your study materials at home or in the hotel room.

E. Expect the Unexpected

No matter how much you have prepared, something unexpected can happen. Urban myths are chock full of "bar exam stories": earthquakes disrupting exams, broken heaters leading to sauna-like exam conditions, students breaking out in hives, students running screaming from the exam room, rock bands banging away next door … Your testing center is likely to have some distractions you were not expecting. Don't let it rattle you. Expect the unexpected. Deal with it. Ignore it. Focus on the exam.

F. Do Not Discuss the Exam

If you followed my advice from first year, don't ignore it now. During the exam, do not discuss specific bar exam questions with others. You will be tempted to do so, but don't do it. Discussing the substance of bar exam will only lead to increasing your stress. Keep your conversations generic.

G. Don't Obsess

When it's over, forget about the exam. You will have answered some questions right and some questions wrong. You didn't need to ace the exam to pass, and students are terrible at predicting whether they passed or not. So don't even try. This is not the time to second guess how you did. In fact, do not think about the exam again until the results are released (several months later). If you have the flexibility, this is a good time to take a vacation. At the very least, try not to go back to work the very next day. You'll be tired. Maybe even exhausted. This is the time to rest. You've earned it.

* * * * *

Basic Preparation for the Bar Exam

☐ Focus and work hard in law school (all three years, not just the first!)

☐ Take any preparation programs that the school offers

☐ Figure out the exam's structure (how many essays, MBE questions, or performance tests)

☐ Pay close attention to application deadlines

☐ Prepare financially and meet with school's financial aid office

☐ Research the different kinds of commercial bar preparation courses available

☐ Clear the decks after graduation to study only for the Bar Exam

Studying for the Bar Exam

☐ Take a preparation courses (not optional, a must!)

☐ Do exactly what the preparation course tells me to do

☐ Create a study schedule for the two months leading up to the exam—and stick with it

☐ Study ten to twelve hours a day (sometimes more)

☐ Study actively (lots and lots of practice exams)

☐ Take times practice exams

☐ Study in a quiet, distraction free place

☐ Stay healthy—eat and exercise

☐ Rely on friends and family

Writing Bar Exam Essays

☐ Use IRAC

☐ Allocate time between questions

☐ Use headings and subheadings

☐ Approach the exam methodically (read the call, read the facts, outline an answer)

☐ Explain your conclusions—use the word "because"

☐ Argue both sides

☐ Move on to next question when allocated time is up (even if not finished)

Practicalities Before the Exam

☐ Reserve a hotel room well in advance

☐ Tie-up loose ends; get personal life in order

☐ Visit the exam site

☐ Pack ahead of time

☐ Figure out where to eat lunch, dinner at exam site

The Day of the Exam

- ☐ Wear comfortable clothes
- ☐ Eat lunch, breakfast and dinner (need food to think properly)
- ☐ Arrive to exam early
- ☐ Leave study materials at home (no cramming!)
- ☐ Prepare mentally to expect the unexpected
- ☐ Never discuss the substance of the exam with friends
- ☐ Don't obsess once it's over

Conclusion

What? You want more? Are you kidding me?! Time to graduate. I got another group of kiddies to start working with. I don't have time to babysit you for your whole life. Grow up.

Appendix A

Selected Bibliography

A. General Advice

Ann Burkhart & Robert Stein, *Law School Success in a Nutshell* (2d ed. 2008)

Atticus Falcon, *Planet Law School II: What You Need to Know (Before You Go), But Didn't Know to Ask, and No One Else Will Tell You* (2d ed. 2003)

Ursula Furi-Perry, *Law School Revealed: Secrets, Opportunities, and Success!* (2009)

Rebecca Fae Greene, *Law School for Dummies* (2003)

Jeremy B. Horwitz, *Law School Insider: The Comprehensive 21st Century Guide* (2002)

Ann L. Iijima, *The Law Student's Pocket Mentor: From Surviving to Thriving* (2007)

Andrew J. McClurg, *1L of a Ride: A Well-Traveled Professor's Roadmap to Success in the First Year of Law School* (2008)

Robert H. Miller, *Law School Confidential: A Complete Guide to the Law School Experience By Students, For Students* (2004)

Gary A. Munneke, *How to Succeed in Law School* (4th ed. 2008)

Shana Connell Noyes & Henry S. Noyes, *Acing Your First Year of Law School: The Ten Steps to Success You Won't Learn in Class* (2d ed. 2008)

Herbert Ramy, *Succeeding in Law School* (2006)

Steven Sedberry, *Law School Labyrinth: A Guide to Making the Most of Your Legal Education* (2009)

Helene Shapo & Marshall Shapo, *Law School Without Fear: Strategies for Success* (2d ed. 2002)

B. Final Exams

Barbara K. Bucholtz et al., *The Little Black Book: A Do-It-Yourself Guide to Law Student Competitions* (2002)

Charles Calleros, *Law School Exams: Preparing and Writing to Win* (2007)

John C. Dernbach, *Writing Essay Exams to Succeed* (2006)

Richard Michael Fischl et al., *Getting to Maybe: How to Excel on Law School Exams* (1999)

Charles H. Whitebread, *The Eight Secrets to Top Exam Performance in Law School* (2d ed. 2007)

C. Learning and Reading

Ruth Anne McKinney, *Reading Like a Lawyer: Time-Saving Strategies for Reading Law Like an Expert* (2005)

Elizabeth Mertz, *The Language of Law School: Learning to Think Like a Lawyer* (2007)

Michael Hunter Schwartz, *Expert Learning for Law Students* (2d ed. 2008)

D. Miscellaneous

Jay M. Feinman, *Law 101: Everything You Need Know About the American Legal System* (2006)

Steven J. Frank, *Learning the Law: Success in Law School and Beyond* (1997)

Rachel Gader-Shafron, *The International Students' Survival Guide to Law School in the United States* (2003)

Kenney F. Hegland, *Introduction to the Study of Law in a Nutshell* (4th ed. 2008)

Linda R. Hirshman, *The Women's Guide to Law School* (1999)

James E. Moliterno & Frederic I. Lederer, *An Introduction to Law, Law Study, and the Lawyer's Role* (2d ed. 2004)

Ruta K. Stopus & Charlotte D. Taylor, *Bridging the Gap Between College and Law School: Strategies for Success* (2d ed. 2009)

Appendix B

Sample Case Brief

A. A Sample Decision

Below is an edited version of the California Court of Appeal decision in *People v. Corson*, 221 Cal. App. 2d 579 (1963). After the decision is a sample case brief.

District Court of Appeal, Third District, California.

The PEOPLE of the State of California, Plaintiff and Respondent,

v.

Harry CORSON, Defendant and Appellant.

Cr. 3484.

Oct. 28, 1963.

Rehearing Denied Nov. 26, 1963.

Defendant was convicted before the Superior Court, Trinity County, Harold Underwood, J., of assault with a deadly weapon, and he appealed. The District Court of Appeal, Schottky, J., held that fact that defendant might have been intoxicated either through use of liquor or mixture of liquor and pills was no defense to prosecution for assault with deadly weapon.

Judgment affirmed.

Harry L. Corson in pro. per.

Stanley Mosk, Atty. Gen., by Doris Maier, Asst. Atty. Gen., and John Giordano, Deputy Atty. Gen., Sacramento, for respondent.

SCHOTTKY, Justice.

Harry Corson was charged by information with the crime of assault with a deadly weapon. He was found guilty as charged by a jury, probation was denied, and judgment was pronounced sentencing him to a term in the state prison. He has appealed from the judgment entered.

The factual situation as shown by the record may be summarized as follows: Corson and his wife lived in a house on a ranch owned by Melvin Senna in Trinity County. On the morning of September 4, 1961, Corson and his wife took a truck of Senna's to go into town to attend to certain errands. When the Corsons failed to return, Senna went to town to learn the cause of the delay. Senna found his truck **586 parked outside a bar. He went to the entrance and saw Corson and his wife sitting at the bar and he told them he was taking the truck. Mrs. Corson came out and asked for a ride back to the ranch. Corson came out and attempted to pull his wife from the vehicle. Senna pulled Corson away. Senna returned to his *581 ranch. About 6:30 p. m. Howard Palmer drove Corson to his house on the ranch. Palmer then drove his car up the road to where Senna was standing and told Senna and Mrs. Corson, 'Harry's really pushed out of shape. [H]e's going to shoot you.' Senna then saw Corson come out of his house armed with a double barreled shotgun. Corson shouted that he was going to kill the 'Portugee.' He broke the gun when he shouted and loaded it. Corson then started walking toward Senna. Senna got into Palmer's truck and was driven to his cabin. He entered his house, got his rifle and returned to the front porch, where he shouted to Corson to stop. Corson continued to walk toward Senna with the shotgun pointed in Senna's direction. Senna fired a warning shot over Corson's head and told Corson not to come any closer. Corson turned around and walked back to his house. When Senna fired the shot Corson was about 175 feet away. The deputy sheriff who arrested Corson testified that he found Corson's shotgun loaded with two shells.

Corson testified in his own defense. The main point of his testimony was that he had taken six pain or nerve pills during the day; that he had not eaten anything; that he drank beer and was pretty drunk. He contended he blacked out. He testified that he could not recollect picking up his shotgun, loading it or walking toward Senna. Corson claimed that the first he could recall was the firing of the shot. He recalled telling Senna he missed and turning around. His next recollection was the arrival of the deputy sheriff.

Section 245 of the Penal Code makes it a crime to commit an assault upon the person of another with a deadly weapon or instrument.

[1] An assault is an unlawful attempt, coupled with a present ability, to commit a violent injury on the person of another. Pen.Code, sec. 240.) To constitute an assault there must be a specific intent to commit a battery, and an act which is close to accomplishment and not mere preparation. (1 Witkin, Cal. Crimes, Assault, sec. 256, p. 242.)

Appellant has filed a brief in propria persona and makes a number of contentions, the first of which is that the evidence is not sufficient to support the conviction of assault with a deadly weapon because, so he contends, there is no evidence that appellant had any intention of causing anybody great bodily injury.

[2][3][4] The applicable law is set forth in People v. Roshid, *582 'All that is required to sustain a conviction of assault with a deadly weapon is proof that there was an assault, that it was with a deadly weapon, and that the defendant intended to commit a violent injury on another. Pen.Code, §245; People v. Marcus, 133 Cal.App.2d 579, 581, 284 P.2d 848. An assault is an unlawful attempt, coupled with a present ability, to commit a violent injury on the person of another. Pen.Code, §240. A gun capable of being fired is a deadly weapon. People v. Pittullo, 116 Cal.App.2d 373, 376, 253 P.2d 705. The intent may be inferred from the doing of the wrongful act. People v. Walker, 99 Cal.App.2d 238, 242, 221 P.2d 287.' (See also People v. McCoy, 25 Cal.2d 177, 189, 153 P.2d 315.)

[5][6] We think it is clear there was ample evidence that there was an unlawful attempt, coupled with the present ability, to commit a violent injury on the person of Mr. Senna. The record indicates that the appellant came out of his house carrying a shotgun. Standing on the porch in full view of

Mr. Senna, Mr. and Mrs. Palmer and Mrs. Corson, the appellant loaded the gun, yelled that he was going to kill the 'Portugee,' and then started walking toward Mr. Senna in a 'stalking' manner **587 and only halted when Mr. Senna finally fired a warning shot into the air. There clearly was an assault. The loaded shotgun in question is well within the meaning of 'deadly weapon or instrument' of section 245 of the Penal Code.

Appellant further contends that due to his intoxicated condition he could not have had any intent to injure Mr. Senna. The law is clear that the intent necessary in this type of case may be inferred from the doing of the wrongful act. (citations omitted)

[7][8] The fact that the appellant may have been intoxicated either by the liquor he consumed or by a mixture of the liquor and the 'pills' he claims he took is no defense. 'No act committed by a person while in a state of voluntary intoxication is less criminal by reason of his having been in such condition.' (Pen.Code, sec. 22.) Voluntary intoxication, whether induced by liquor or drugs, is not a defense. (Citations Omitted).

The judgment is affirmed.

PIERCE, P. J., and FRIEDMAN, J., concur.

B. Case Brief

PEOPLE v. CORSON
34 Cal. Rptr. 584 (Ct. App. 1963)

ISSUE:

Under California law, is a defendant guilty of assault with a deadly weapon when he grabs a double-barreled shotgun, loads it, and shouts that he is "going to kill the [victim]" before being stopped, if at the time the defendant is intoxicated after drinking beer and taking pain pills?

FACTS:

Corson lived with his wife on a ranch that Senna owned. One day Corson took Senna's truck to town. When Corson did not return, Senna investigated and found Corson drinking at a bar. Corson had taken six pain pills, had not eaten anything, and drank beer until he "was pretty drunk." Senna drove the truck and Corson's wife back to the ranch.

That evening, after Corson returned to the ranch, he came out of his house armed with a double-barreled shotgun. Corson loaded the gun, and shouted to Senna that he was going to kill him. Corson then started walking in a "stalking manner" towards Senna. Senna had previously been told that Corson was "really pushed out of shape.... [and was] going to shoot [Senna]." Senna retrieved his own gun, shot a warning shot over Corson's head, and told Corson not to come any closer. Corson turned around and walked back to his house. Later, Corson was arrested.

PROCEDURE:

Corson was charged with, convicted of, and sentenced for assaulting Senna with a deadly weapon. Corson appealed. He contended: (1) that his actions did not constitute assault because there was no evidence he intended to cause anyone great bodily injury; and (2) because of his intoxication, he could not have had the intent to injure Senna.

LEGAL RULES:

1. Assault is an unlawful attempt, coupled with a present ability, to commit a violent injury. Cal. Penal Code §240. 2. Committing an assault with a deadly weapon or instrument is a crime. Cal. Penal Code §245. 3. "No act committed by a person while in a state of voluntary intoxication is less criminal by reason of his having been in such a condition." Cal. Penal Code §22.

HOLDING:

A loaded shotgun is within the meaning of "deadly weapon or instrument" of section 245, and there was sufficient evidence of intent. That the defendant might have been voluntarily intoxicated is no defense to prosecution for assault.

REASONING:

First, a gun capable of being fired is a deadly weapon. Second, carrying a shot gun, loading it, threatening to kill a person, and then walking towards that person is ample evidence of an intent to injure another. Under the statute and case-law, voluntary intoxication is not a defense.

Appendix C

Sample Final Exam

A. Sample Exam Question

CIVIL PROCEDURE ESSAY

(Suggested Time: 75 min.)

In October 2009, while visiting New York, Pam and her sister were injured when their car collided with Abe's car after Abe ran a red light. Pam, who was her sister's passenger, suffered significant pain in her neck, including bruising and swelling. Pam did not see a doctor. A week later, after Pam returned to California, Pam was in another car collision. This time the accident was between Pam and Bella. The collision occurred because Bella was speeding and talking on her cell phone. After the accident, Pam was diagnosed with a hairline cervical fracture (i.e., a minor break of a neck bone). The doctor was unable to determine whether the first or second car accident caused the fracture.

Pam and her sister sued Abe and Bella in one action. Pam asserted negligence claims seeking $100,000 from each defendant. Pam's sister asserted a negligence claim against Abe for $75,000. Pam and her sister filed the suit in a California federal court. Pam alleged in her complaint that both accidents caused her neck injury. Pam and her sister are California citizens, while Abe and Bella are New York citizens. Abe has never been to California. He has no friends or family there. He has never done any business in California and does not own property there.

Abe intended to take a week vacation in Seattle starting on December 1, 2009, so Abe booked a direct, non-stop flight from New York to Seattle. A month before the flight, the airline notified Abe by e-mail that the flight would no longer be direct: the plane would land in San Francisco before continuing on to Seattle. Abe never saw the e-mail, however, and did not learn of the stop until after the flight left New York. Pam, however, learned that Abe would be landing in San Francisco and hired a process server. The plane landed in San Francisco and the process server boarded the plane (he had bought a ticket for the flight from San Francisco to Seattle). While the plane was still grounded in California, the process server served Abe with the summons and complaint.

Abe filed three motions to dismiss with the court. Abe's first motion contended that under the Federal Rules of Civil Procedure Abe and Bella may not be joined as co-defendants in the same lawsuit. He further argued that the claims against him should be dismissed for misjoinder. Abe's second motion asserted that the court did not have subject matter jurisdiction over the sister's claim against Abe. Abe's third motion asserted that the court did not have personal jurisdiction over him. The court denied all three of Abe's motions.

Please answer the following three questions:

1. Did the court correctly decline to dismiss the claims against Abe and find that he and Bella were properly joined as co-defendants? (35 pnts)
2. Did the court correctly find it had subject matter jurisdiction over the sister's claim against Abe? Federal question jurisdiction does not exist for any claim in the lawsuit and you should not discuss that basis for jurisdiction. (25 pnts)
3. Did the court correctly find it had personal jurisdiction over Abe? (40 pnts)

B. Sample Exam Answer

CIVIL PROCEDURE ESSAY EXAM
Sample Essay Exam Answer

---

1. Did the court correctly decline the motion to dismiss and find that Abe and Bella were properly joined as co-defendants?

The question raises two issues. Do the Federal Rules of Civil Procedure permit joinder and was the court correct in denying Abe's motion to dismiss.

A.   May plaintiffs join Abe and Bella as co-Defendants?

Parties may be sued as co-defendants if two requirements are met. First, the asserted right to relief must arise from the same transaction and occurrence or series of transactions or occurrences. Second, a question of law or fact common to both defendants must exist.

1.   Same Transaction or Occurrence

In determining whether claims arise from the same transaction or occurrence or series of transactions or occurrences, courts often apply the logical relation test. Claims are logically related if separate trials on each of the claims would involve a substantial duplication of effort and time by the parties and the courts.

Here, the accidents do not seem logically related because they occurred at different times (a week apart), in different places (New York versus California), and involved different people (Abe versus Bella). In the first accident, Pam was not driving. The second accident involved a different driver (Pam) in a different car. The causes of the accidents were also different (speeding/talking on phone versus running a red light). Because the accidents occurred a week apart and in different parts of the country, the witnesses (such as any emergency responders, police, fire, etc., and any bystanders) would be presumably different. Because the accidents occurred in different states, the substantive law and choice of law rules may also be different, which has the potential to confuse the jury if the case was heard together.

On the other hand, courts have tended to interpret Rule 20 broadly and many have expanded the notion of transactional relatedness through tort theories. Courts are often flexible, making a common-sense assessment as to whether joinder in a single case is fair and consistent with the liberal joinder policy underlying the Federal Rules. Some courts have found that when an injury has two causes and the harm attributable to each cause is indeterminable that it's appropriate to view the same transaction requirement satisfied. The court might view the "occurrence" as the broken neck, and therefore both claims arise from the same occurrence (the breaking of the neck). A court may also conclude that a series of occurrences—the two accidents—caused Plaintiff's injury. Also because the plaintiff and the injury are the same, the evidence related to the damages and causation will be the same.

A strong policy consideration exists for hearing both claims together. Should the cases not be heard together the plaintiff may be "whipsawed." A whipsawed plaintiff may well convince two juries that she is entitled to recovery, but end up with nothing, since each jury believed the absent defendant was the responsible party. Said differently, each defendants may point fingers at the defendant not before the court claiming that the absent party caused the injury. The result could be that the innocent plaintiff recovers from neither defendant. Also the claims are fairly straightforward negligence claims from a simple event (a car accident)—so a jury should be easily able to understand the key issues if the two claims are combined. Given the congestion in the courts and the desire to reduce litigation, a court is likely to err on the side of permitting claims to be joined when doing so would be efficient.

Given the possible unfairness of allowing a plaintiff to be whipsawed, the desire for efficiency and the reduction of multiplicity of actions, as well as the flexibility underlying the rules, this element was likely satisfied.

2. Common Question of Law or Fact

The requirement that claims involve common questions or law or fact usually does not present a difficulty when claims are transactionally related. Questions common to both lawsuits in this case include: what caused the neck injury and what was the extent of Pam's injuries/damages. There might also be common issues surrounding any alleged contributory negligence on Pam's part. Therefore this element is satisfied.

B. Should the claims against Abe be dismissed?

Even if the Abe and Bella were not properly joined, the court was correct not to dismiss. Misjoinder is not a basis for dismissing an action. The remedy for misjoinder is to sever. (Rule 21). Severance results in two separate suits, each with its own docket number and judgment. Here Abe sought dismissal for misjoinder — exactly what Rule 21 prohibits. Therefore the court was correct in denying the motion to dismiss.

2. Did the court correctly find it had subject matter jurisdiction over the sister's claim against Abe?

Federal courts are courts of limited jurisdiction. If a court does not have original jurisdiction (here diversity, since the question says federal question does not exist), it must have supplemental jurisdiction to hear the claim.

A. Did the court have diversity jurisdiction?

For a court to have diversity jurisdiction two requirements must be satisfied: (1) that complete diversity of citizenship exists (i.e., that the plaintiffs and defendants are citizens of different states); and (2) that the amount in controversy exceeds $75,000.

The parties are completely diverse because the facts state that the sister is a California citizen and Abe is a New York citizen. But the second element — the amount in controversy — is not met. The sister is suing for exactly $75,000, and therefore the statutory requirement that the dispute be *for more* than $75,000 has not been met. Because the complaint is for less than the required amount, the defendant can establish to a legal certainty that plaintiff failed to meet the amount-in-controversy requirement.

Nor can the sister meet the amount in controversy requirement by aggregating her claim with Pam's claim. Multiple plaintiffs may not aggregate separate and distinct claims. The only exception is if the plaintiffs hold a common and undivided interest (e.g., ownership of a common fund or partnership). In this case, there is no common and undivided interest. For one, the damages are easily separated. Pam's injury is to her neck, while her sister is not seeking recovery for Pam's injured neck but presumably her own injuries and the damage to her car. Also the claims have been separated (Pam seeks $100,000, while the sister seeks $75,000). No facts are given that would suggest somehow the claims of Pam and her sister are the same.

Because the amount in controversy has not been met, diversity jurisdiction does not exist over the sister's claim.

B.   Did the court have supplemental jurisdiction?

Even if the court lacks original jurisdiction over all claims, it will be able to hear the jurisdictionally insufficient claim if supplemental jurisdiction exists. A court may have supplemental jurisdiction over closely related claims (1367(a)), so long as the claim is not by a plaintiff against a party joined under FRCP Rules 14, 19, 20 or 24 (1367(b)).

1.   1367(a) — Relatedness Analysis

The sister's claim is closely related to Pam's claim. Claims are sufficiently related to form one case or controversy under Article III if they arise from a common nucleus of operative facts. (1367(a) and *Gibbs*). Here, Pam and her sister were injured in a car accident with Abe. They were in the same car together when the accident occurred and were injured at the same time. Pam's and her sister's injuries arise from the same event — Abe running a red light. Therefore the court will find the claims arose from the same operative facts.

2.   1367(b) — Supplemental Analysis in Diversity Cases

The court is barred from exercising supplemental jurisdiction, however, under 1367(b). When the basis for original jurisdiction is in diversity, supplemental jurisdiction does not exist if the claim is: (1) by a plaintiff; and (2) against a part joined under Rules 14, 19. 20 or 24.

In this case, the court may not exercise supplemental jurisdiction. First, Pam's claim against Abe (the anchor claim) sounds in diversity. The facts say there exists no federal question jurisdiction, that Pam and Abe are citizens of different states (California v. New York) and that the amount in controversy is over $75,000 (Pam is suing for $100,000). Second, this is a claim by a plaintiff. The facts tell us that the sister is a plaintiff suing Abe. Third, this is a claim against a party joined under Rule 20. The facts say that the sister is suing Abe, and the analysis from question #1 above shows that Abe and Bella are joined under Rule 20 as co-defendants. Because the requirements of 1367(a)(2) carve-out are met, the court does not have supplemental jurisdiction over this claim. The court was probably mistaken in not granting Abe's second motion to dismiss.

3. Did the court correctly find it had personal jurisdiction over Abe?

Both a statutory and a constitutional analysis is required to determine whether a court has personal jurisdiction.

A. Long Arm Statute Analysis

In a federal court, jurisdiction is limited by FRCP Rule 4(k). That rules say that federal courts must apply the long-arm of the state in which the federal court sits. Here the case is pending before a California federal court. The California long-arm statute extends California court's jurisdiction to the fullest extent permitted under the U.S. Constitution . Therefore if the exercise of jurisdiction is constitutional the long-arm requirements are also met.

B. The Constitutional Analysis

The 14th Amendment's Due Process Clause limits a court's authority to enter judgments against defendants who has insufficient connections to the forum in which the court sits. Because Abe was personally served while physically present within the forum state (here California), the issue is whether tag jurisdiction exists (under

Burnham). The Supreme Court has been unclear, however, as to the basis for tag jurisdiction and courts have taken two analytical approaches.

1. A Territorial Theory of Jurisdiction (Scalia)

Under one approach (set forth by Scalia in *Burnham*), jurisdiction exists whenever a defendant is physically present in the state and is personally served. Under this territorial theory of jurisdiction, the basis for jurisdiction lies in the English tradition and American common law—dating before the landmark *Pennoyer* case—which found that every state may rightfully exercise jurisdiction over persons within its territory. While case like *International Shoe* (and later *Shaffer v. Heitner*) meant that states would not be bound to adhere to the unbending territorial limits set forth in *Pennoyer*, transitory presence remains a basis of jurisdiction consistent with the due process standard. Under this analytical approach, jurisdiction based on physical presence alone does not violate due process and therefore need not be subjected to the International Shoe minimum contacts analysis.

If the court adopts the territorial theory of jurisdiction, the facts say that Abe was personally served when in San Francisco. Because Abe was served while in California, jurisdiction is established. The fact that Abe was in the state for a brief period of time is irrelevant: personal service upon a physically present defendant suffices to confer jurisdiction regardless of whether the defendant is only briefly in the state. Nor is it relevant under a territorial theory whether the defendant was in the state voluntarily. Cases have found that jurisdiction is proper even when the defendant is in the state involuntarily. See, e.g., *People v. Williams* (personal jurisdiction over person involuntarily confined to state hospital). Under a territorial theory—the mere presence alone is sufficient. Even if voluntariness was an issue, no facts exist to suggest that Abe was forced into the state or entered in voluntarily (in the sense of being tricked).

2. A Modern Approach (Brennan)

But courts have also applied a second analytical approach to tag jurisdiction (set forth by Brennan in *Burnham*). Under this second approach, all forms of jurisdiction must comport with modern notions of due process. Although in-state service will often meet these requirements, a categorical rule does not exist. This is particularly true when a defendant is present in a forum involuntarily. When the defendant is in the state for a particularly brief period of time this also suggests that the exercise of jurisdiction may be unreasonable.

Under this approach, it's unlikely that jurisdiction should exist. Jurisdiction under the modern approach exists only if the defendant has minimum contacts with the forum so that the exercise of jurisdiction comports with traditional notions of fair play and substantial justice. Here, exercising jurisdiction over a defendant who is not purposefully in the state, and remains in the state for a very short period of time, on matters unrelated to the lawsuit seems unreasonable.

Under the modern approach, jurisdiction is unlikely. Specific jurisdiction exists over claims that arise from a defendant's forum activity, so long as the defendant has purposefully availed itself of the privileges and benefits of the forum state. Specific jurisdiction will not exist because Abe's landing in San Francisco (his contact with California) did not give rise to the lawsuit (i.e., the accident, which occurred a month earlier in New York). Nor did Abe purposefully avail himself of the benefits of California, since he did not reach out and deliberately get involved in a car accident with a California citizen. He did not intend or plan to be in California at all: the facts say he did not realize he was going to land in California until after he boarded the plan.

General jurisdiction also does not exist. General jurisdiction exists when a defendant has continuous, systematic and substantial contacts with a state. Because the facts say that Abe has never been to California, has no family or friends there, has never done business in California, and does not own property there, the court could not find Abe to have continuous, systematic or substantial contacts. The exercise of jurisdiction would also be unreasonable (not comporting with traditional notions of fair play and substantial justice) given the short period of time Abe spent in the state, the lack of any attempt to use California services, the fortuity of service on Abe and the hardship of him having to travel to defend in California. In *Burnham* jurisdiction was found on very slim connections, but the connections here are slimmer still.

3. A Reconciliation

It is unclear which approach the court should apply. On the one hand, the territorial approach that Scalia has described might lead to greater predictability, efficiency, and consistency. It creates a bright-line rule that is easy to apply and reduces judicial discretion and ad hoc decisions. Predictability in procedure is important because it allows defendants to conform their behavior. Also the U.S. Supreme Court has turned more conservative in recent years, and Scalia's historical approach may be attractive to other members of the Court.

On the other hand, the territorial approach, like any categorical rule, can be wooden and lead to unfair results in some cases. In this particular case, the territorial approach seems to unnecessarily burdens Abe with fortuitous assertions of jurisdiction. Certainly jurisdiction in this context seems inconsistent with the idea that jurisdiction should limit a court's power to hear cases involving defendants with little connections to the forum, or that a defendant must have done something "purposefully" to have a connection with the forum. Tag jurisdiction for transient defendants is also inconsistent with the approach used in many other countries and some commentators have argued violates international law. Lastly, the territorial approach is very hard to reconcile with the court's earlier decisions in *Shaffer* and *International Shoe*.

The courts have been split in which approach they take. On balance, however, given that the car accident occurred in New York and the witnesses and evidence is there, and because Abe did not intend to visit California and was served only fortuitously, jurisdiction seems unlikely.

About the Authors

Austen L. Parrish: Professor Parrish is the Vice-Dean and a Professor of Law at Southwestern Law School. He is also the co-director of the school's Summer Law Program at the University of British Columbia in Vancouver, B.C., Canada. Professor Parrish teaches courses in Civil Procedure, Civil Pretrial Practice, Federal Courts, International Environmental Law, and Public International Law. While his scholarship focuses primarily on transnational legal issues, he has also taught courses in legal writing and appellate advocacy, and has lectured in the school's academic support program. He is the co-author of *Effective Lawyering: A Checklist Approach to Legal Writing and Oral Argument*.

Professor Parrish earned his B.A. from the University of Washington, in Seattle, and his J.D. from Columbia Law School, where he was a Harlan Fiske Stone Scholar. While at Columbia, he served as a Managing Editor of the Columbia Journal of Transnational Law and as a student editor of the Columbia Journal of European Law. Prior to entering academia, Professor Parrish was an attorney in the litigation department of O'Melveny & Myers.

In addition to teaching at Southwestern, Professor Parrish has taught at Loyola Law School in Los Angeles, and has lectured for the commercial bar review preparation course Personal Bar Prep. He is a faculty advisor to the *Southwestern Journal of International Law* and has received awards for his work with Southwestern's Moot Court Honors Program. In 2007, Professor Parrish was honored with the school's excellence in teaching award, and the Irwin R. Buchalter Professorship.

Cristina C. Knolton: Professor Knolton is an Associate Professor of Legal Writing, Analysis and Skills at Southwestern Law School. Prior to joining Southwestern, Professor Knolton taught at Texas Tech University School of Law and LaVerne College of Law. In addition to legal writing and analysis, Professor Knolton has taught the subjects of negotiation, alternative dispute resolution, property, and marital property.

Professor Knolton is currently the co-director of the Negotiation Honors Program at Southwestern and coaches Southwestern's ABA National Negotiation team. In 2007, Professor Knolton was nominated for the Hemphill-Wells New Professor Teaching Award. She has spoken before academic and professional forums on topics such as "Incorporating Exams into the Legal Writing Classroom," "How to Succeed in Law School," "Texas Community Property Law," "A Lawyer's Role as an Advocate in the Legal System," and "Negotiation Tactics in Criminal Defense."

After completing her law degree at the University of Texas, where she was a member of the Texas Law Review, Professor Knolton began her legal career as a real estate attorney at the firm of Akin, Gump, Strauss, Haeur & Feld in San Antonio, Texas, representing commercial real estate clients in the acquisition, sale, ownership, and leasing of income-producing properties. She has also served as a volunteer mediator for the Lubbock County Alternative Dispute Resource Center.

Index